Edwin Hodder

A Book of Uncommon Prayers

Literary, biographical, historical

Edwin Hodder

A Book of Uncommon Prayers
Literary, biographical, historical

ISBN/EAN: 9783337012281

Printed in Europe, USA, Canada, Australia, Japan

Cover: Foto ©ninafisch / pixelio.de

More available books at **www.hansebooks.com**

A Book of Uncommon Prayers.

A Book of Uncommon Prayers

Literary
Biographical
Historical

Compiled by
Edwin Hodder

AUTHOR OF "CONQUESTS OF THE CROSS,"
"SIMON PETER: HIS LIFE AND TIMES,"
"ON HOLY GROUND," ETC., ETC.

London
J. S. Virtue and Co., Ltd.
26, Ivy Lane, E.C.
1898.

Preface.

THERE are almost innumerable collections of sacred poetry and hymns—there are comparatively few collections of prayers.

"A good prayer," says worthy Thomas Fuller, "is not, like a stratagem of war, to be used but once. No: the oftener the better. The clothes of the Israelites, whilst they wandered forty years in the wilderness, never waxed old. So a good prayer, though often used, is still fresh and fair in the ears and eyes of Heaven. Despair not then, thou simple soul, who hast no exchange of raiment; whose prayer cannot appear every day at Heaven's court in new clothes. Only add new, or new degrees of old affections thereunto, and it will be acceptable to God, thus repaired, as if new created."

In these days of restless activity—when men have no leisure, no repose, little inducement and less opportunity for prayerful contemplation—it has been found that in what brief intervals in the strain and struggle of life can be obtained, much spiritual help and refreshment have been gained in reading the devout thoughts, the aspirations, the hopes, the fears of men of all generations who, in prayer, have talked with God.

It is quite true that the literature of prayer may be made conventional and common-place, and that a long series of prayers composed by one person, may become a book of mere repetitions, but it is equally true that in the selected prayers of men of large hearts and wide influence who have left their mark on the history of the Church in times of critical importance in the past, no less than in the prayers of thoughtful men in the changing and unstable present, there are to be found valuable gems of devout expression, deep and wondrous thoughts of God and man, fruitful aids from rich experience, and rousing words of hope and aspiration.

I have endeavoured, therefore, to select *Uncommon* prayers—some on the ground of their literary excellence, others for their biographical or historical interest, and the majority for the depth of their devotional spirit.

Good prayers, like good hymns of praise, will live as long as the world, and will bear witness to the true communion of saints in all ages and in all lands.

I have great pleasure in acknowledging the generous assistance I have received from my friends the Rev. James Durran, M.A. (Edinburgh), the Rev. Thomas Nicholson, M.A. (Bromley, Kent), Mr. J. M. Grant, J.P., and Mr. John Angell James Housden, in pointing out to me valuable sources of information while this work was in progress.

I tender my cordial thanks to Mrs. Elmslie for kindly placing at my disposal the MS. prayers (Nos. 102, 103, 104, 105), hitherto unpublished, of her late husband, Professor W. Gray Elmslie, M.A., D.D.; to Dr. Alexander Whyte for permission to use the prayers Nos. 10, 23, and 24; Dr. James Martineau for Nos. 92 and 107; the Earl of Lovelace and Messrs. Isbister and Co., Ld., for No. 72; Messrs. Macmillan and Co. for No. 73; the Rev. J. V. Charlesworth for No. 94; Dr. J. Oswald Dykes and Messrs. Jas. Nesbit and Co., Ld., for No. 96; Mrs. Service and Messrs. Macmillan and Co. for Nos. 98 and 99; Dr. Joseph Parker (City Temple) for Nos. 100 and 101; and to Messrs. I. MacLehose and Sons (Glasgow) for No. 108.

I have used my best endeavours to discover the owners of the copyrights of all prayers included in this volume, but if in any instance I have inadvertently made use of a prayer for which I should have obtained the permission so willingly extended in other cases, I tender my apology, and shall be glad to rectify the error in any subsequent editions.

EDWIN HODDER.

HEATHERDENE,
   HARBWOOD ROAD,
      SOUTH CROYDON.

Contents.

	Page.
PREFACE	v

Thoughts on Prayer.

(1) DEFINITIONS OF PRAYER	1
(2) ANSWERS TO PRAYER	5
(3) DUTY OF PRAYER	8
(4) POWER OF PRAYER	13
(5) NECESSITY OF PRAYER	16
(6) DELIGHT AND CONSOLATION IN PRAYER	19

Prayers.

No.	Author.	Date.	Subject.	Page
I.	St. Polycarp . . .	A.D. 163	Immediately before his Martyrdom . . .	24
II.	St. James	200	A General Prayer . . .	25
III.	St. Jerome . . .	329-420	For Private Use before Communion	26
IV.	St. Augustine . .	354-430	For Rest in God	29
V., VI.	St. Basil	379	Two Collects	31—32
VII.	John Damascenus .	676-756	The Cry of the Contrite Soul	33
VIII.	Simeon Metaphrastes	10th cent.	An Acrostic Prayer . . .	35
IX.	St. Thomas Aquinas	1224-1274	Before Communion . . .	36
X.	Archbishop Bradwardine . .	1290-1349	A Private Prayer . . .	38
XI.	Thomas à Kempis .	1380-1471	For Peace of Mind . . .	39
XII.	Dean Colet . . .	1466-1519	A Family Prayer . . .	42
XIII.	John Knox . . .	1505-1572	In Time of Persecution and Trial	44
XIV.	St. Francis Xavier .	1506-1552	Adoration	45
XV.	John Calvin . . .	1509-1564	A Morning Prayer . . .	46
XVI.	,,	,,	An Evening Prayer . . .	47
XVII.	,,	,,	Before Communion . . .	49
XVIII.	,,	,,	Confession	50
XIX.	Martin Luther . .	1521	Before Appearance at Diet at Worms	51
XX.	Vittoria Colonna .	1541	For Spiritual Life . . .	53

No.	Author.	Date.	Subject.	Page.
XXI.	Vittoria Colonna	1543	For Renewal of Spiritual Life	54
XXII.	Sir Walter Raleigh.	1552-1618	A Hymn of Prayer	54
XXIII.	Bishop Lancelot Andrewes	1555-1626	A Prayer on Awaking	55
XXIV.	Bishop Lancelot Andrewes	,,	An Evening Prayer for Grace	58
XXV.	Sir Henry Wotton	1568-1639	Prayer in a Night of Sickness	60
XXVI.	Archbishop Laud	1573-1645	A Family Prayer	61
XXVII.	Ben Jonson	1574-1637	To the Holy Trinity	62
XXVIII.	Bishop Hall	1574-1656	A Private Prayer	64
XXIX.	Jacob Böhme	1575-1624	A Prayer of Contrition	65
XXX.	Robert Herrick	1591-1674	A Litany to the Holy Spirit	68
XXXI.	George Herbert	1593-1632	"The Elixir"	70
XXXII.	Queen Elizabeth	1597	For the Nation	71
XXXIII.	King Charles I.	1600-1649	A Family Prayer	72
XXXIV.	Jeremy Taylor	1613-1667	Prayer for the Graces of Faith, Hope, and Charity	74
XXXV.	,,	,,	A General Prayer	76
XXXVI.	Drummond of Hawthornden	1617	A Prayer for Mercy	77
XXXVII.	Richard Baxter	1615-1691	A General Prayer	78
XXXVIII.	Blaise Pascal	1623-1662	In Time of Sickness	81
XXXIX.	Dr. John Donne	1631	A Litany	82
XL.	,,	,,	A Hymn to God the Father	84
XLI.	,,	,,	A Prayer in Sickness	84
XLII.	Francis Quarles	1635	The Hiding of God's Face	86
XLIII.	,,	,,	A Private Prayer	88
XLIV.	Johann Lassenius	1636-1692	An Evening Prayer	89
XLV.	Bishop Ken	1637-1711	A Prayer of Thanksgiving	91
XLVI.	Henry Vaughan	1650	"Begging"	93
XLVII.	Bishop Wilson	1663-1755	A Private Prayer	94
XLVIII.	Andrew Rykman	1674	,,	95
XLIX.	William Law	1686-1761	,,	101
L.	Philip Doddridge	1702-1751	For Divine Guidance in Dispensing Gifts	102
LI.	Dr. Samuel Johnson	1709-1784	On Preparing for Study	103
LII.	,,	,,	Against Inquisitive and Perplexing Thoughts	104
LIII.	,,	,,	Before Communion	105
LIV.	Moravian Brotherhood	1722	A Prayer for Missions	106
LV.	Gerhard Tersteegen	1724	A Prayer of Self-Dedication	107
LVI.	,,	1731	To the Risen and Ascended Saviour	108
LVII.	Alexander Pope	1734	The Universal Prayer	111
LVIII.	John Burn of Glasgow	1738	A Covenant Prayer	114
LIX.	Charles Wesley	1740	A Hymn of Private Prayer	116

Contents.

No.	Author.	Date.	Subject.	Page.
LX.	Susanna Wesley	1742	On the Love of God	117
LXI.	Thomas Chatterton	1752-1770	Resignation	118
LXII.	Robert Southey	1774-1843	A Prayer	119
LXIII.	Bishop Mant	1776-1848	A Litany	120
LXIV.	Thomas Moore	1779-1852	Bereavement	121
LXV.	Sir Robert Grant	1785-1838	A Litany	121
LXVI.	Dr. Thomas Arnold	1795-1842	The Prayer of a Busy Man	123
LXVII.	,,	,,	6th Form Morning Prayer at Rugby	123
LXVIII.	John Greenleaf Whittier	1807-1892	For Peace and Calm	124
LXIX.	Elizabeth Barrett Browning	1809-1861	The Cry of the Human	125
LXX.	Dr. Thomas Chalmers	1816	On Friendship	129
LXXI.	Dr. Thomas Chalmers	,,	In Time of Plague	131
LXXII.	Mrs. John Sheppard	1821	A Prayer for Lord Byron	133
LXXIII.	Matthew Arnold	1822-1888	"Save, oh ! save"	136
LXXIV.	Sir John Bowring	1825	A Hymn of Prayer	139
LXXV.	Adolphe Monod	1826	A Cry from the Depths	140
LXXVI.	Bishop Heber	,,	Prayer for Conversion	141
LXXVII.	Rev. Richard Knill	1829	The Old and New Year	142
LXXVIII.	Principal Forbes	1830	On Coming of Age	143
LXXIX.	,,	,,	After Sickness and Sorrow	143
LXXX.	Rev. Alexander Fletcher	1834	A Morning Family Prayer	144
LXXXI.	Henry Thornton, M.P.	1834	,,	147
LXXXII.	James Russell Lowell	1841	Prayer for a Life	150
LXXXIII.	Abbé Lacordaire	1846	On Preaching Christ	150
LXXXIV.	Eliza Cook	1849	Evening Prayer for the Sick and Sorrowful	151
LXXXV.	Sir Robert Peel	1850	A Statesman's Prayer	152
LXXXVI.	Sir Henry Lawrence	1852	For the Duties of the Day	153
LXXXVII.	Rev. E. B. Pusey, D.D	1853	A Morning Prayer	154
LXXXVIII.	John Sheppard of Frome	,,	For Assurance of Faith	158
LXXXIX.	John Sheppard of Frome	,,	For Pardon under Distressing Doubt	160
XC.	Dr. James Hinton	1859	Some Thoughts on Prayer	162
XCI.	London School Board	1870	Used at Meetings of First London School Board	163
XCII.	Miss Frances Power Cobbe	1871	For the Indwelling of God	166
XCIII.	Prince Imperial of France	1879	Prior to Departure for Zululand	168
XCIV.	Rev. C. H. Spurgeon	1878	A Pulpit Prayer. Extempore	170

Contents.

No.	Author.	Date.	Subject.	Page.
XCV.	Rev. H. W. Beecher	1813-1887	A Pulpit Prayer. Extempore	178
XCVI.	Dr. J. Oswald Dykes	1881	For the Last Evening of the Year	187
XCVII.	Seventh Earl of Shaftesbury	1885	Special Prayers	190
XCVIII.	Dr. John Service	,,	General Prayer for Public Worship	193
XCIX.	,,	,,	At the Burial of the Dead	200
C.	Dr. Joseph Parker	1889	A Family Prayer	203
CI.	,,	,,	,,	205
CII.	Professor W. Gray Elmslie, D.D.	,,	General Prayer for Public Worship	206
CIII.	Professor W. Gray Elmslie	,,	For Restoration of the Divine Likeness	210
CIV.	Professor W. Gray Elmslie	,,	Two Prayers of Invocation	212
CV.	Professor W. Gray Elmslie	,,	A Prayer of Intercession	213
CVI.	Benjamin Jowett, Master of Balliol	1891	A College Prayer in Illness	214
CVII.	Dr. James Martineau	,,	For Morning or Evening	216
CVIII.	Dr. John Hunter	1895	For Sunday Morning in Autumn	218
CIX.	. . . .	. . .	A Prayer for the Use of the Young People of a Household	221
CX.	. . . .	. . .	A Little Child's Prayer	224
CXI.	The Blind Chaplain of the American Senate	1897	For the Queen	225

INDEX OF AUTHORS QUOTED 226

SUBJECT INDEX 227

A Book of Uncommon Prayers.

Thoughts on Prayer.

(1) Definitions of Prayer.

PRAYER, if I may speak so boldly, is intercourse with God. Even if we do but lisp, even though we silently address God without opening our lips, yet we cry to Him in the inmost recesses of the heart; for God always listens to the sincere direction of the heart to Him.—*Clement of Alexandria.*

Prayer is the meeting-point of the seen and the unseen; it is the borderland between earth and heaven; it is the contact and communion of finite beings with the Infinite.—*Dr. Huntingdon.*

Prayer is not the synonym of petition—prayer is speaking to God whatsoever be the voice, the language, the subject of discourse. It may be confession, it may be adoration, it may be thanksgiving, it may be petition. If it be petition it may be entreaty, it may be deprecation, it may be intercession, it may be for the life, it may be for the soul. . . prayer is the soul's language in the ear of a God known to be present. A man may pray who asks nothing, who but "dwells in the secret place of the Most High"—silent petition, counting it enough to abide under the shadow of the Almighty, the All-Loving. The reality of prayer is the meeting of the two spirits, the "I," and the "I Am," unto communication, unto converse, unto interchange (with reverence be it spoken) of thought and speech, of life and love.—*Very Rev. C. J. Vaughan, D.D.*

> Heaven is the magazine wherein God puts
> Both good and evil; prayer's the key that shuts
> And opens this great treasure; 'tis a key
> Whose wards are Faith, and Hope, and Charity.
> —*Francis Quarles.*

Prayer is helplessness casting itself upon power; it is infirmity leaning on strength, and misery wooing bliss; it is unholiness embracing purity, hatred desiring love; it is corruption panting for immortality, and the earth-born claiming kindred in the skies; it is the flight of the soul to the bosom of God, and the spirit soaring upward and claiming nativity beyond the stars; it is the restless

Definitions.

dove on drooping wing turning to its loved repose; it is the soaring eagle mounting upward in its flight, and with steady gaze pursuing the track till lost to all below; it is the roving wanderer looking toward his abiding-place, where are all his treasures; it is the prisoner pleading for release; it is the mariner on a dangerous sea upon the reeling topmast, descrying the broad and quiet haven of repose; it is the soul oppressed by earthly soarings, escaping to a broader and a purer sphere, and bathing its plumes in the ethereal and eternal. — *Thornton Wells.*

> Prayer is the soul's sincere desire,
>   Uttered or unexpressed;
> The motion of a hidden fire
>   That trembles in the breast.
>
> Prayer is the burthen of a sigh,
>   The falling of a tear,
> The upward glancing of the eye,
>   When none but God is near.
>
> Prayer is the simplest form of speech
>   That infant lips can try;
> Prayer the sublimest strains that reach
>   The Majesty on high.
>
> Prayer is the Christian's vital breath,
>   The Christian's native air.
> His watchword at the gate of death;
>   He enters heaven with prayer.
>   —*James Montgomery.*

Prayer draws all the Christian graces into its focus; it draws charity, followed by her lovely train—her forbearance with faults, her forgiveness of injuries, her pity for errors, her compassion for want. It draws repentance with her holy sorrows, her pious resolutions, her self-distrust; it attracts faith with her elevated eye; hope, with her grasped anchor; beneficence, with her open hand; zeal looking far and wide to serve; humility with introverted eye, looking at home. Prayer, by quickening these graces in the heart, warms them into life, fits them for service, and dismisses each to its appropriate practice.—*Mrs. Hannah More.*

>Prayer is a culture of the soul,
>   That turns to wheat our tares;
>Prayer is a begging angel, whom
>   We shelter unawares.
>
>Prayer is a wisdom which the wise
>   To babes have oft resign'd,
>But He who bade us seek, be sure
>   He meant that we should find . . .
>
>A small hand feeling in the night,
>   A natural gasp for air,
>A half-articulate aim at speech—
>   To want to pray is prayer.
>   —*J. B. Monsell.*

(2) Answers to Prayer.

God often answers the prayer of His people, as He did the seed of Isaac, with a hundredfold increase. As His word never returns empty to Him, so the prayers of His servants never return empty to them; and usually the crop of prayer is greater than the seed out of which it grew; as the putting in of a little water into a pump makes way to the drawing out of a great deal more.—*Bishop Reynolds.*

God delays to answer prayer, because He would have more of it. If the musicians come to play at our doors or our windows, if we delight not in their music, we throw them out money presently that they may be gone. But if the music please us, we forbear to give them money, because we would keep them longer to enjoy their music. So the Lord loves and delights in the sweet words of His children, and therefore puts them off and answers them not presently.—*Archbishop Usher.*

Prayer flies where the eagle never flew, and rises on wings broader and stronger than an angel's. It travels further and faster than light. Rising from the heart of a believer, it shoots away beyond that starry sky, and, reaching the throne, enters into the ear of God. So soon as the heart begins to work on earth, it moves the hand of God in heaven; and ere the prayer has left the lips of faith, Jesus has presented it to His Father, and secured its answer.—*Dr. Thomas Guthrie.*

You account it a good answer to a petition when you have that which is better than the thing desired; but when you desire that which is not good, the denial is better than the grant. These denials are great mercies, and hence sweet returns of prayer.—*Rev. David Clarkson.*

> So weak is man,
> So ignorant and blind, that did not God
> Sometimes withhold in mercy what we ask,
> We should be ruin'd at our own request.
> —*Hannah More.*

> We, ignorant of wisdom,
> Beg often our own harms, which the wise powers
> Deny us for our good; so find we profit
> By losing of our prayers.
> —*Shakespeare.*

God sometimes delays the answer that it may be more beneficent when it comes. The stream is made to turn and wind that it may receive contributions

from every valley which it passes, and all to flow more largely into the bosom at last. When God's plans ripen slowly, it is that the fruit may be the richer and mellower. Hence it is that the royal munificence of His bounty knows no limits at last.
—*James McCosh, LL.D.*

    Thy prayer shall be fulfilled; but how?
      His thoughts are not as thine,
  While thou wouldst only weep and bow,
      He saith "Arise and shine!"
  Thy thoughts were all of grief and night,
  But His of boundless joy and light.

  Thy Father reigns supreme above;
      The glory of His name
  Is Grace and Wisdom, Truth and Love.
      His will must be the same.
  And thou hast asked all joys in one,
  In whispering forth "Thy Will be done!"
               —*Frances Ridley Havergal.*

  Pray! though the gift you ask for
  May never comfort your fears;
  May never repay your pleading,—
  Yet pray, and with hopeful tears!
  An answer; not that you long for,
  But diviner,—will come some day;
  Your eyes are too dim to see it,
  Yet strive, and wait and pray.
              —*Adelaide Proctor.*

(3) The Duty of Prayer.

Prayer has always been recognised as one of the duties of natural religion. In all ages and among all nations it has been common, by some form or rite, to supplicate divine protection and favour. Among the golden verses of Pythagoras we find the following:—

> In all thou dost, first let thy prayers ascend,
> And to the gods thy labours first commend!
> From them implore success, and hope a prosperous end.
> —*W. Fleming.*

Prayer is not a duty to be entered upon rashly and without preparation. If we pass into the Almighty's presence reeking, as it were, of the earth, not pausing on the threshold to compose and solemnise the mind by a deliberate act of reflection and examination, it can hardly be wondered at that we find slight, if any, comfort, in drawing nigh unto our Father who is in Heaven.—*H. Melville, B.D.*

A man cannot be a true believer, a child of God, unless he be a man of prayer. For what the breath is to the body, prayer is to the soul. If the breath gasp and be faint, the body grows out of order; and, if prayer be slack and unfrequent, the soul becomes diseased. If breath ceases, life is at an end; and, if prayer ceases, all hope for the soul perishes. As soon as we give over communing with God, Satan enters in and begins to commune with us. Man can never walk alone. If he choose not the better part to walk with his God, he must choose to walk with God's adversary and his own. Oh that man would but be persuaded—"Prayer is man's best work."—*Martin Luther.*

Let prayer be the key of the morning, and the bolt of the evening.—*Matthew Henry.*

Prayer has the power of sanctifying life, because it brings God into life. Twice in the day it has been for ages the habit of the race to use this talisman, once for the sanctification of the day, once for the sanctification of the night. The morning prayer chimes in with the joy of the creation, with the quick world, as it awakes and sings. Such a prayer is the guard of life. It makes us conscious of our Father's presence, so that we hear His voice in the hour of our folly and our sin: "My child, this morning you called Me to your side; do not drive Me away. Bridle that passionate temper, restrain that excitement which is sweeping you beyond the power of will; keep back that foolish word which will sting your neighbour's heart; do not do that dishonesty; be not guilty of that cowardice, I am by your side."— *Stopford Brooke.*

> Be not afraid to pray—to pray is right.
> Pray if thou canst, with hope; but ever pray,
> Though hope be weak, or sick with long delay:
> Pray in the darkness, if there be no light.
> Far is the time, remote from human sight,
> When war and discord on the Earth shall cease.
> Yet every prayer for universal peace
> Avails the blessed time to expedite.
> Whate'er is good to wish, that ask of Heaven,
> Though it be that thou canst not hope to see;
> Pray to be perfect, though material leaven
> Forbid the spirit so on earth to be!
> But if for any wish thou darest not pray,
> Then pray to God to cast that wish away.
> —*Hartley Coleridge.*

> Who goes to bed and doth not pray,
> Maketh two nights of every day.
> —*Geo. Herbert.*

> Men ought always to pray and not to faint.
> —*St. Luke,* xviii. 1.

As God knows all things, it is not in order that He may be informed of our wants that He has appointed prayer, nor is it to dispose and incline

Him to show mercy, because God in Christ Jesus is self-moved by His love to His people to do this, but there are three principal reasons why God requires prayer in order to the bestowment of mercies on men. First, thereby to acknowledge our dependence on Him; for as God has made all things for His glory, so He will be glorified and acknowledged by His people especially, and it is fit He should require this of those who would be the subjects of His mercy. Second, to exercise and strengthen the Christian graces. Prayer tends to strengthen faith, to increase love, humility, and patience, to invigorate hope, and benefit all the graces of the Spirit in the real believer; and the more he prays in faith, the more all these graces grow. And, thirdly, God requires prayer to make us more sensible of the value of the mercies we seek. If we were to have favours without asking for them, such is our depravity that we should think too lightly of them; but by being made to wait for them, and kept, by faith, in expectation of receiving them, when they come they are generally better received. Hereby is excited a sense of our need of the mercies we pray for, and the mind is better prepared to prize them when received, and to rejoice and be thankful for them when bestowed. Thus we have the greatest reason to bless the Lord that He has made prayer a duty, and we should pray that it may be made our delight.—*President Edwards.*

    What wondrous grace! who knows its full extent?
    A creature, dust and ashes, speaks with God;
    Tells all his woes, enumerates his wants,
    Yea, pleads with Deity, and gains relief.
    'Tis prayer, yes, 'tis effectual, fervent prayer
    Puts dignity on men, proves life divine,
    Makes demons tremble, breaks the darkest cloud,
    And, with a princely power, prevails with God.
    And shall this privilege become a task?
    My God forbid! Pour out Thy Spirit's grace,
    Draw me by love, and teach me how to pray.
    Yea, let Thy holy unction from above
    Beget, extend, maintain my intercourse,
    With Father, Son, and Spirit, Israel's God,
    Until petitions are exchanged for praise.
                  —*Rev. Prebendary Irons.*

        Prayer was not meant for luxury
          Or selfish pastime sweet;
        It is the prostrate creature's place
          At his Creator's feet.
                —*Faber.*

Serve God before the world: let Him not go
Until thou hast a blessing; then resigne,
The whole unto Him: and remember who
Prevailed by wrestling ere the sun did shine.
   Pour oyle upon the stones; weep for thy sinne,
   Then journey on, and have an eie to heaven.
                       H. Vaughan.

> More things are wrought by prayer
> Than this world dreams of. Wherefore, let thy voice
> Rise like a fountain for me night and day.
> For what are men better than sheep or goats,
> That nourish a blind life within the brain,
> If, knowing God, they lift not hands of prayer,
> Both for themselves and those who call them friend ?
> For so the whole round world is every way
> Bound by gold chains about the feet of God.
> —*Tennyson.*

(4) The Power of Prayer.

Religion is the bond between the soul and God, which sin, by virtue of its very nature, breaks and destroys. It is of importance to inquire whether man can strengthen and intensify that which he can, it seems, so easily ruin if he will. Does his power lie only in the direction of destruction? Has he no means of invigorating and repairing a tie in itself so precious, yet in some respects so frail? The answer lies in our Lord's promise: "Ask, and it shall be given unto you." Prayer is the act by which man, conscious at once of his weakness and of his immortality, puts himself into real and effective communication with the Almighty, the Eternal, the self-existent God.—*Canon Liddon.*

> Then, fainting soul, arise and sing!
> Mount! but be sober on the wing;
> Mount up: for Heaven is won by prayer.
> Be sober, for thou art not there.
> —*Keble.*

Sometimes a fog will settle over a vessel's deck, and yet leave the topmast clear. Then a sailor goes up aloft and gets a look-out which the helmsman on deck cannot get. So prayer sends the soul aloft; lifts it above the clouds in which our selfishness and egotism be-fog us, and gives us a chance to see which way to steer.—*C. H. Spurgeon.*

Prayer does not directly take away a trial or its pain, any more than a sense of duty directly takes away the danger of infection, but it preserves the strength of the whole spiritual fibre, so that the trial does not pass into the temptation of sin.—*Stopford Brooke.*

It is said of Archimedes, that famous mathematician of Syracuse, who having by his art framed a curious instrument, that if he could but have told how to fix it, it would have raised the very foundations of the whole earth. Such an instrument is prayer, which, if it be set upon God and fixed in heaven, will fetch earth up to heaven, change earthly thoughts into heavenly conceptions, turn flesh into spirit, metamorphose nature into grace, and earth into heaven.—*Venatorius.*

>Prayer moves the Hand which moves the world.
>   —*J. A. Wallace.*

> Lord, what a change within us one short hour
>   Spent in Thy presence will prevail to make;
>   What heavy burdens from our bosoms take;
> What parched grounds refresht as with a shower!
> We kneel, and all around us seems to lower;
>   We rise, and all—the distant and the near—
>   Stands forth, in sunny outline, brave and clear.
> We kneel; how weak! We rise; how full of power!
> Why, therefore, should we do ourselves this wrong,
> Or others, that we are not always strong?
>   That we are ever overborne with care,
> That we should ever weak or heartless be,
>   Anxious or troubled, when with us in prayer,
> And joy, and strength, and courage are with Thee?
>   —*Trench.*

Would you measure in some sort the gains of this communion with God to which we are admitted and invited, consider only what we may gain by communion with good and holy men, and then conclude from this less to the greater. Consider the elevating, ennobling influences which it exercises on the character to live in habitual intercourse with the excellent of the earth, with those whose conversation is in heaven, tones of whose minds are high, and lofty, and pure. Almost without being aware of it, we derive some of their spirit into ourselves; it is like an atmosphere of health which we unconsciously inhale. But how much more must this be the case, how far weightier the reactive influence for good, when we continually set before us, when we live in fellowship with Him, who is the highest, the purest, and the best; in whom all perfections meet, from whom all true nobleness proceeds: when thus our fellowship is not with men, who have caught a few glimpses of the glory of God, but with God Himself, from whom all greatness and glory proceeds.—*Archbishop Trench.*

(5) The Necessity of Prayer.

As familiar conversation (wherein men do express their minds and affections mutually) breedeth acquaintance, and cherisheth goodwill of men to one another, but long forbearance thereof dissolveth or slackeneth the bonds of amity, breaking their intimacy, and cooling their kindness; so it is in respect to God; it is frequent converse with Him that begetteth a particular acquaintance with Him,

Necessity of Prayer.

a mindful regard of Him, a hearty liking to Him, a delightful taste of His goodness, and consequently a sincere and solid goodwill toward Him; but intermission thereof produceth estrangement or enmity toward Him. If we seldom come to God, we shall little know Him, not much care for Him, scarce remember Him, rest insensible of His love, and regardless of His favour; a coldness, a shyness, a distaste, an antipathy toward Him will by degrees creep upon us. Abstinence from His company and presence will cast us into conversations destructive or prejudicial to our friendship with Him; wherein soon we shall contract familiarity and friendship with His enemies (the world and the flesh) which are inconsistent with love to Him, which will dispose us to forget Him, or to dislike and loathe Him.—*Isaac Barrow.*

When you have given over the practice of stated prayer, you gradually become weaker without knowing it. Samson did not know he had lost his strength till the Philistines came upon him. You will think yourselves the men you used to be, till suddenly your adversary will come furiously upon you, and you will as suddenly fall.—*Cardinal Newman.*

A prayer in an hour of pain,
   Begun in an undertone,
Then lowered, as it would fain
   Be heard by the heart alone !—
A throb, when the soul is entered
   By a light that is lit above,
Where the God of Nature has centered
   The Beauty of Love !—
The world is wide,—these things are small,
They may be nothing, but they are All.
                      —*Houghton.*

No soul can preserve the bloom and delicacy of its existence without lonely musing and silent prayer; and the greatness of this necessity is in proportion to the greatness of the soul. There were many times during our Lord's ministry when, even from the loneliness of desert places, He dismissed His most faithful and most beloved, that He might be yet more alone.—*Archdeacon Farrar.*

It is because we are God's children, not merely His creatures, that He will have us pray. Because He is educating us to know Him; to know Him, not merely to be an Almighty Power, but a living, loving Person; not merely an irresistible Fate, but a Father who delights in the love of His children, who wishes to shape them into His own likeness, and make them fellow-workers with Him. There-

Delight in Prayer.

fore it is that He will have us pray. Doubtless He *could* have given us everything without our asking: for He *does* already give us almost everything without our asking. But He wishes to educate us as His children; to make us trust in Him; to make us love Him; to make us work for Him of our own free wills, in the great battle which He is carrying on against evil; and that He can only do by teaching us to pray to Him. I say it reverently, but firmly. As far as we can see, God cannot educate us to know Him, the living, willing, loving Father, unless He teaches us to open our hearts to Him, and to ask Him freely for what we want, just *because* He knows what we want already.—*Charles Kingsley.*

> Thrice blest, whose lives are faithful prayers,
>   Whose lives in higher love endure!
> What souls possess themselves so pure?—
>   Or is there blessedness like theirs?
>   —*Tennyson.*

(6) **Delight and Consolation in Prayer.**

> My God! is any hour so sweet;
>   From blush of morn to evening star,
> As that which calls me to Thy feet,
>   The hour of prayer!

Blest be that tranquil hour of morn,
  And blest that hour of solemn eve,
When, on the wings of prayer upborne,
        The world I leave.

For then a dayspring shines on me,
  Brighter than morn's ethereal glow;
And richer dews descend from Thee,
        Than earth can know.

Then is my strength by Thee renewed,
  Then are my sins by Thee forgiven,
Then dost Thou cheer my solitude,
        With hopes of heaven.

Words cannot tell what sweet relief
  Here for my every want I find,
What strength for warfare, balm for grief,
        What peace of mind.

Hushed is each doubt, gone every fear,
  My spirit seems in heaven to stay;
And e'en the penitential tear
        Is wiped away.
            —*Charlotte Elliott.*

Speak to Him thou, for He hears, and spirit with spirit can meet;
Closer is He than breathing, and nearer than hands and feet.
            —*Tennyson.*

Go thou into thy closet; shut thy door—
  And pray to Him in secret: He will hear.
  But think not thou, by one wild bound, to clear
The numberless ascensions; More and more

> Of starry stairs that must be climbed, before
>   Thou comest to the Father's likeness near;
>   And bendest down to kiss the feet so dear
> That, step by step, their mounting flights passed o'er.
>   Be thou content if on thy weary need
> There falls a sense of showers and of the Spring;
>   A hope that makes it possible to fling
>   Sickness aside, and go and do the deed;
>   For higher aspiration will not lead
> Unto the calm beyond all questioning.
>   —*Geo. MacDonald.*

Prayer is to the penitent heart a sweet source of consolation, long even before the answer come; because a generous mind rejoices in acknowledging the obligations it desires to receive, or has received; or the faults, errors, and offences which it has committed; and a candid mind delights in holy unburdenings, and an humble mind in the confession of its own incapacity for doing good; all which sentiments accompany penitential prayer. And, also, that the exercise itself is a drawing nigh unto One who giveth liberally and upbraideth not. God has no frowns for the penitent; He hears their cry, and will help them.—*Rev. J. S. Knox.*

There is something in the very act of prayer that for a time stills the violence of passion, and elevates and purifies the affections. When affliction presses hard, and the weakness of human nature looks around in vain for support, how natural is the impulse that throws us on our knees before Him who has laid His chastening hand upon us, and how encouraging the hope that accompanies our supplications for His pity. We believe that He who made us cannot be unmoved by the sufferings of His children; and in sincerely asking his compassion we almost feel that we receive it.—*Jeremy Taylor.*

> When hearts are full of yearning tenderness
> For the loved absent, whom we cannot reach
> By deed, or token, gesture, or kind speech,
> The spirit's true affection to express;
> When hearts are full of innermost distress,
> And we are doomed to stand inactive by,
> Watching the soul's or body's agony,
> Which human effort helps not to make less,—
> Then, like a cup capacious to contain
> The overflowings of the heart, is prayer;
> The longing of the soul is satisfied,
> The keenest darts of anguish blunted are;
> And though we cannot cease to yearn or grieve,
> Yet we have learned in patience to abide.
> —*Trench.*

> "They who have steeped their souls in prayer
>   Can every anguish calmly bear—
> They who have learnt to pray aright
>   From pain's dark well draw up delight."
>   Your words are fair,

But oh! the truth lies deeper still!—
I know not—when absorbed in prayer—
Pleasure or pain, or good or ill;
They who God's face can understand,
Feel not the motions of His hand.
—*Houghton.*

Conclusion.

If we with earnest effort could succeed
To make our life one long connected prayer,
As lives of some perhaps have been and are;
If—never leaving Thee—we had no need
Our wandering spirits back again to lead
Into Thy presence, but continued there,
Like angels standing on the highest stair
Of the sapphire throne,—this were to pray indeed.
But if distractions manifold prevail,
And if in this we must confess we fail,
Grant us to keep at least a prompt desire,
Continual readiness for prayer and praise—
An altar heaped and waiting to take fire
With the least spark, and leap into a blaze!
—*Trench.*

Prayers.

I.—Prayer of St. Polycarp, Martyr Bishop of Smyrna, as he stood beside the stake awaiting his fate. A.D. 163.

O LORD GOD, Father Almighty, the Father of Thy well-beloved and ever-blessed Son Jesus Christ, by whom we have received the knowledge of Thee; the God of angels, powers, and of every creature, and of the whole race of the righteous who live before Thee, I thank Thee that Thou hast graciously thought me worthy of this day and of this hour, that I may receive a portion in the number of Thy martyrs, and drink of Christ's cup for the resurrection to immortal life, both of body and soul, in the incorruptibleness of the Holy Spirit, among whom may I be admitted this day as a rich and acceptable sacrifice, as Thou, O true and faithful God, hast prepared, and foreshown, and accomplished. Wherefore I praise Thee for all Thy mercies: I bless Thee, I glorify Thee with the eternal and heavenly Jesus Christ, Thy beloved Son, to whom with Thee and the Holy Spirit be glory now and for ever. Amen.

II.—A Prayer from the Liturgy of St. James. PRIOR TO A.D. 200.

[The Liturgy of Jerusalem, popularly called after St. James, is the parent of St. Basil's, and so of St. Chrysostom's, and of a great number of Syrian forms.]

O God, the Father of our Lord God and Saviour Jesus Christ, Lord, Whose name is great, Whose nature is blissful, Whose goodness is inexhaustible, Thou God and Master of all things, Who art blessed for ever; Who sitteth on the Cherubim, and art glorified by the Seraphim, before Whom stand thousands of thousands, and ten thousand times thousands, the hosts of holy angels and archangels: sanctify, O Lord, our souls and bodies and spirits, and touch our apprehensions, and search out our consciences, and cast out of us every evil thought, every base desire, all envy and pride and hypocrisy, all falsehood, all deceit, all worldly anxiety, all covetuousness, vain-glory, and sloth, all malice, all wrath, all anger, all remembrance of injuries, all blasphemy, and every motion of the flesh and spirit that is contrary to Thy holy will. And grant us, O Lord, the Lover of men, with freedom, without condemnation, with a pure heart and a contrite soul, without confusion of face and with sanctified lips, boldly to call upon Thee our holy God and Father who art in Heaven. Amen.

III.—A Prayer for Private use before Holy Communion. By St. Jerome. 329-420.

[St. Jerome, a Father of the Latin Church, born in Dalmatia, died at Bethlehem. His Latin version of the Old Testament, from the original language, was the foundation of the Vulgate.]

Behold, O my God, I am the man who went down to Jericho and fell among thieves; sorely have they wounded me and left me lying half-dead. Come, Lord, Thou faithful Helper, raise me up and heal me.

I have sinned heavily in my whole conduct, and done evil in Thy sight; I have not exercised myself in the knowledge of Thee; I have been unthankful for Thy many benefits, and have not praised Thy name aright. Often and in many ways have I abstained from uttering Thy truths, and when Thou hast stood and knocked at the door of my heart I have been slothful, and have not welcomed Thee as I ought. This body, which fadeth like a shadow, and shall be the food of worms, I have cherished too much; I have defiled my lips with unseemly words, and I have been negligent and careless about

Thy wholesome Word. I have not ever and always turned away my eyes from beholding vanity, nor kept my ears from listening to unprofitable things. Many a time my hands have not served my neighbour in his need, while my feet were swift to evil. What need I say more, my God? From the crown of my head to the sole of my feet there is no health in me.

Ah! my Lord Jesus, hadst Thou not died for me on the Cross, and redeemed me, my soul must have perished for ever; but now am I a partaker, O merciful Lord, in Thy great salvation. O reject not one, my Saviour, whom Thou hast so dearly purchased with Thy precious blood. Behold, I am a wandering sheep, seek me, Thou good Shepherd, and bear me home to Thy fold, according to Thy promise. Thou hast promised, O my Helper, that whenever a poor sinner shall sigh unto Thee Thou wilt hearken unto him. Now see how humbly I mourn and acknowledge my sins, which are ever before me. In truth, I am not worthy to be called Thy son, yet make me, my Saviour, to hear joy and gladness, and turn not away Thy face from me.

O Thou Son of the Living God, Only Begotten of Thy Father before all worlds! blessed are those who love Thee and desire naught else; blessed are those who daily remember Thee and keep Thy ways unto their life's end. O Holy Bread of Heaven, how rich and bounteous art Thou; how overflowing are Thy gifts! For Thou excludest no man unless it be that he despises Thee and refuses to come to Thee. Is anyone young and small, let him come boldly to Thee and eat, and he will grow and increase; he will put away his childish mind, and walk in the paths of true wisdom. Is any yet weak, let him hasten to Thee and eat and he shall soon wax strong. Is any sick, he shall be relieved. Is any dead in sins, let him but hearken to Thee and he shall attain everlasting life. And though one be strong and full grown, yet will he perceive that he is still in need of many things, and in Thee will he find abundantly that whereby he may daily increase in them. None can live a moment without Thee, for it is Thou alone who givest life to all creatures. O God, the joy and consolation of my heart, my soul is glad in Thee, and my spirit hath a desire unto Thee; for all who turn away from Thee must pine for ever. O Thou true and invisible Light which never can be quenched, behold me sitting like a poor blind man beside the way, and crying unto Thee, " Jesus, Thou Son of David, have mercy upon me, open the eyes of my soul, that I may see Thee! Lord, be merciful to me, a sinner. Thou art my Help and my Confidence, oh lead me unto eternal salvation! Lord, Thou art my physician, heal me! I am naked, and suffer cold, O Thou rich Lord, cover me with the mantle of Thy righteousness. My soul hungers in this desert; do Thou, Lord, the true Food, quicken my heart. My soul is athirst. Lord, Thou art the true healing Spring, water and refresh my spirit with Thy wholesome comfort. I am come into the deep mire, and my strength faileth me; I am far out on the seas, and the floods threaten to swallow me up. I have cried till I am weary and hoarse, and the waters of death are coming into my very soul. Save me, O Lord, my Shield, my Deliverer, my Comfort, my Refuge, my Strength, my King and my God, for Thy mercies' sake. Amen.

IV.—A Prayer for Rest in God. By St. Augustine. 354-430.

[St. Augustine, a renowned Father of the Christian Church, was born at Tagaste, in Africa. His mother, Monica, was a Christian; his father, Patricius, a pagan. He became a convert of St. Ambrose, Bishop of Milan, by whom he was baptised. In 395 he became Bishop of Hippo. "He was a man of great enthusiasm, self-devotion, zeal for truth, and powerful intellect, and though there have been Fathers of the Church more learned, none have wielded a more powerful influence."]

Thee, O Lord, who fillest the heavens and the earth; Thee Who upholdest all things by Thine everpresent might: Thee, most merciful God, do I now invoke to descend into my soul which Thou hast prepared for Thy reception by the desire which Thou hast breathed into it. Enter into it and renew it in Thy likeness that Thou mayest possess it, and that I may have Thee as a seal upon my heart. Ere ever I cried to Thee, Thou, most Merciful, hadst called and sought me, that I might find Thee, and finding, love Thee. Even so I sought and found Thee, Lord, and desire to love Thee. Increase my desire, and grant me what I ask. Bestow Thyself upon me, my God. Yield Thee unto me: see I love Thee but too little; strengthen my love: let love to Thee alone influence my heart, and let the thought of Thee be all my joy. When my spirit aspires to Thee, and meditates on Thine unspeakable goodness, the burden of the flesh becomes too heavy, the tumult of thought is still, the weight of mortality is less oppressive. Then fain would my soul find wings, that she may rise in tireless flight ever upwards to Thy glorious throne, and there be filled with the refreshing solace that belongs to the citizens of heaven. Let my soul thus ever seek Thee and never grow weary of seeking; for he who seeketh Thee not is miserable, and he who refuses to live to Thee is dead. Therefore, O Thou full of Compassion, do I commit and commend myself unto

Thee, in Whom I am, and live, and know. May my soul be occupied with Thee only. Be Thou the goal of my pilgrimage, and my rest by the way. Let my soul take refuge from the crowding turmoil of worldly thoughts beneath the shadow of Thy wings; let my heart, this sea of restless waves, find peace in Thee, O God. Thou bounteous giver of all good gifts, give to him who is weary refreshing food; gather our distracted thoughts and powers into harmony again, and set the prisoner free. See, he stands at Thy door and knocks; be it opened to him, that he may enter with a free step and be quickened by Thee. For Thou art the Well-spring of Life, the Light of Eternal Brightness wherein the just live who love Thee. Be it unto me according to Thy word! Amen.

V.—Collect. By St. Basil. 379.

[St. Basil, called the *Great*, a well-known Father of the Greek Church, was born in 329, and in 370 was made Bishop of Cæsarea, in Cappadocia, where he died in 379. He was the author of several prayers, and compiled a Liturgy still in use in the East. The Greek Church honours him as one of its most illustrious Saints, and celebrates his festival on January 1.]

Eternal God, Thou self-existent Light, which wast from the beginning; Maker of all creatures, Fountain of mercy, Ocean of goodness, Thou fathomless Abyss of loving-kindness; suffer now the light of Thy countenance to arise upon us! Shine into our hearts, O Thou true Sun of righteousness, and fill our souls with Thy beauty. Teach us evermore to think and talk of Thy judgments and acknowledge Thee at every moment as our Lord and our Benefactor. Direct according to Thy will the work of our hands, and lead us in the right way to do that which is pleasing in Thy sight; so that through us, unworthy though we be, Thy Holy Name may be glorified, the Name of the Father, the Son, and the Holy Ghost, to whom alone be praise, honour and glory for ever and ever. Amen.

VI.—Another Collect. By St. Basil. 379.

O Lord our God, who hast given peace to men, and hast sent down Thy Holy Spirit on Thy apostles and disciples, bestowing on them in Thy power fiery tongues wherewith to speak Thy praise; open also our lips, sinners though we be, and teach us to ask Thee aright for the right blessings. Steer Thou the vessel of our life toward Thyself, Thou tranquil Haven of all storm-tost souls. Show us the course wherein we should go. Renew a willing spirit within us. Let Thy Spirit curb our wayward senses, and guide and ennoble us unto that which is our true good, to keep Thy laws, and in all our works evermore to rejoice in Thy glorious and gladdening presence. Let us not be deluded by the fleeting pleasures of this world, but strengthen us, that we may aspire to the enjoyment of that which is to come. For Thine is the glory and praise from all Thy saints for ever and ever. Amen.

VII.—**A Prayer by John Damascenus.** EARLY IN EIGHTH CENTURY.

"In our selection from the Anacreontic hymn, the tears seem to trickle audibly: we welcome them as a Castalia, or, rather, 'as Siloa's brook,' flowing by an oracle more divine than any Grecian one :—

> From my lips in their defilement,
> From my heart in its beguilement,
> From my tongue which speaks not fair,
> From my soul stained everywhere,
> O my Jesus, take my prayer!
> Spurn me not for all it says,
> Not for words and not for ways,
> Not for shamelessness endued!
> Make me brave to speak my mood,
> O my Jesus, as I would!
> Or teach me, which I rather seek,
> What to do and what to speak.
>
> I have sinnèd more than she,
> Who learning where to meet with Thee,
> And bringing myrrh, the highest-priced,
> Anointed bravely, from her knee,

Thy blessed feet accordingly,
My God, my Lord, my Christ!
As Thou saidest not "Depart,"
To that suppliant from her heart,
Scorn me not, O Word, that art
The gentlest one of all words said!
But give Thy feet to me instead,
That tenderly I may them kiss
And clasp them close, and never miss
With over-dropping tears as free
And precious as that myrrh could be,
T' anoint them bravely from my knee!
Wash me with Thy tears; draw nigh me,
That their salt may purify me.
THOU remit my sins who knowest
All the sinning to the lowest—
Knowest all my wounds, and seest
All the stripes Thyself decreest;
Yea, but knowest all my faith,
Seest all my force to death,
Hearest all my wailings low,
That mine evil should be so!
Nothing hidden but appears
In my knowledge, O Divine,
O Creator, Saviour mine—
Not a drop of falling tears,
Not a breath of inward moan,
Not a heart-beat—which is gone!

After this deep pathos of Christianity, we dare not say a word; we dare not even praise it as poetry; our heart is stirred, and not 'idly.' The only sound which can fitly succeed the cry of the contrite soul, is that of divine condonation or of angelic rejoicing. Let us, who are sorrowful still, be silent too."

ELIZABETH BARRETT BROWNING,
The Greek Christian Poets, 1842.

VIII.—Curious Acrostic Prayer of Simeon Metaphrastes.
CLOSE OF TENTH CENTURY.

Ah, tears upon mine eyelids, sorrow on mine heart,
    I bring Thee soul-repentance, Creator as Thou art!
Bounding, joyous actions, deep as arrows go;
    Pleasures self-revolving, issue into woe!
Creatures of our mortal, headlong rush to sin;
    I have seen them; of them—ah me,—I have been!
Duly pitying Spirits, from your spirit-frame
    Bring your cloud of weeping,—worthy of the same!
Else I would be bolder; if that light of Thine,
    Jesus, quell the evil, let it on me shine!
Fail me truth, is living, less than death forlorn,
    When the sinner readeth—"better be unborn"?
God, I raise toward Thee both eyes of my heart,
    With a sharp cry—"Help me!" while mine hopes depart.
Help me! Death is bitter, all hearts comprehend;
    But I fear beyond it—end beyond the end.
Inwardly behold me, how my soul is black;
    Sympathise in gazing, do not spurn me back!
Knowing that Thy pleasure is not to destroy,
    That Thou fain wouldst save me—this is all my joy.
Lo, the lion, hunting spirits in their deep,
    (Stand beside me!) roareth—(help me!) nears to leap.
May'st Thou help me, Master! Thou art pure alone,
    Thou alone art sinless, one Christ on a throne.
Nightly deeds I loved them, hated day's instead;
    Hence this soul-involving darkness on mine head.

O Word, who constrainest things estranged and curst,
  If Thy hand can save me, that work were the first!
Pensive o'er my sinning, counting all its ways,
  Terrors shake me, waiting adequate dismays.
Quenchless glories many, hast Thou—many a rod—
  Thou, too, hast Thy measures. Can I bear Thee, God?
Rend away my counting from my soul's decline,
  Show me of the portion of those saved of Thine!
Slow drops of my weeping to Thy mercy run:
  Let its rivers wash me, by that mercy won!
Tell me what is worthy, in our dreary now,
  As the future glory? (madness!) what, as THOU?
Union, oh, vouchsafe me to Thy fold beneath,
  Lest the wolf across me gnash his gory teeth!
View me, judge me gently! spare me, Master bland,
  Brightly lift Thine eyelids, kindly stretch Thine hand!
Winged and choral angels! 'twixt my spirit lone
  And all deathly visions, interpose your own!
Yea, my Soul, remember death and woe inwrought—
  After-death affliction, wringing earth's to nought!
Zone me, Lord, with graces! Be foundations built
  Underneath me; save me! as Thou know'st and wilt!

The omission of our X (in any case too sullen a letter to be employed in the service of an acrostic) has permitted us to write line for line with the Greek. . . .

ELIZABETH BARRETT BROWNING,
The Greek Christian Poets, 1842.

IX.—**Prayer of St. Thomas Aquinas.** 1224—1274. BEFORE COMMUNION.

O Almighty and everlasting God, behold I draw near to the Sacrament of Thine only-begotten Son, our Lord Jesus Christ. I draw near as a sick man to the Physician, as one defiled to the Fountain of mercy, as one blind to the Light of the eternal splendour, as one poor and needy to the Lord of heaven and earth. Wherefore I implore the fulness of Thine infinite bounty, that Thou wouldst vouchsafe to heal all my sickness, to wash away my defilement, to give light to my blindness, to enrich my poverty, and to clothe my nakedness, so that I may receive the Bread of Angels, the King of Kings, and Lord of Lords, with such contrition and devotion, such purity and faith, such purpose and intention, as may avail to the welfare and salvation of my soul.

Grant me, I beseech Thee, to receive not only the Sacrament of the Body and Blood of my Lord, but also the very reality and power of the Sacrament. O most gracious God help me so to receive the Body of Thine only-begotten Son, our Lord Jesus Christ, that very Body which He took of the Virgin Mary, that I may be truly incorporated into His mystical Body and so be numbered amongst its members. O most loving Father grant me at last to behold face to face and for evermore the same Thy beloved Son, whom I purpose to receive now in my pilgrimage beneath the veils of the Sacrament, Who liveth and reigneth, &c. Amen.

X.—A Prayer of Thomas Bradwardine, Archbishop of Canterbury. 1290—1349.

[Thomas Bradwardine was perhaps the first Englishman who applied a regular connected series of reasoning from principles, or conclusions already established, to theological subjects, and from this circumstance arose the honourable title, by which he was commonly known, of the profound Doctor—"Doctor Profundus." He was Chaplain and Confessor to Edward III., and attended that monarch during his wars in France. He was elected to the primacy in 1349, but died before he had been enthroned.]

Thyself, my God, I love. Thyself for Thyself, above all things. For Thyself I long. Thyself I desire as a final end. Thyself for Thyself, not for aught else, I always and in all things seek with my heart and whole strength, with groaning and weeping, with continual labour and grief. What, therefore, wilt Thou give me as my final end? If Thou dost not bestow on me Thyself, Thou bestoweth on me nothing. If Thou dost not give me Thyself, Thou givest me nothing. If I find not Thyself, I find nothing. Thou dost not then reward me, but torturest me. For even before that I sought Thee, I hoped to find and possess Thee at last. And with this honeyed hope I was sweetly consoled in all my labours. But now, if Thou deniest me Thyself, and that for ever, and not for a season, whatever else Thou shalt give me, shall I not always languish with love, mourn with languishing, grieve with mourning, weep with grieving, because I shall ever remain void and empty? Shall I not mourn inconsolably, complain unceasingly, grieve interminably? That is not Thy wont, God of goodness, of clemency and of love: it is in no wise fitting, in no point seemly. Grant, therefore, O my gracious God, that in the present life I may ever love Thyself for Thyself above all things, seek Thee in all things, and in the world to come may find Thee and keep hold of Thee for ever. Amen.

<small>Quoted in "Lancelot Andrewes and His Private Devotions." By Dr. Alex. Whyte, p. 224.</small>

XI.—**A Prayer to Obtain the Peace of Mind which Christ gave to His Disciples. By Thomas a Kempis (Haemmerlein).** BORN 1380, DIED 1471.

O Lord Jesu Christ, from whom floweth all that is sweet, King of heaven and earth, the true peace of hearts and comforter of those who mourn, say, I pray Thee, unto my soul, troubled and desolate as Thou fully knowest it to be, "I am thy salvation, thy peace, thy life, thy comfort, thy hope, thy light and thy rest.

"In Me is all thy good, the true solace of the soul, every present and unending joy. What more dost thou desire?"

Nothing, Lord, Thee only do I desire. Thee I

seek, Thee I long for, Thee I dearly love. Thee, in all things and over all things, always and everywhere, I bless and praise.

Thou rulest over all things in heaven and earth, in the sea, and in all great depths; in the mountains and in the woods, and every creature, small and great, is known to Thee and clear before Thee.

In wisdom hast Thou made them all, and by Thy providence are they all governed.

O peace of God, O clear knowledge of my Creator, which passeth all reason and the understanding of men and angels! when wilt Thou come unto me, when wilt Thou fill me within and without, that I may have nothing more to desire?

O Lord God, my heart is disquieted until it may rest in Thee. My mind cannot be at peace until it be perfectly one with Thee in Life eternal. O peace! how sweet and desirable is Thy name in all the earth!

How joyful and how pleasant is Thy voice in the heavenly country, O true, sovereign, everlasting peace, with God, with the holy angels, and with men of holy will.

Grant me peace in my heart, O Lord, that I may fully love Thee. Grant me peace in my mouth, that I may devoutly praise Thee. Grant me peace in my hand, that I may ever do all good works to Thy honour.

Say unto me when I am in heaviness, "Peace be unto thee; it is I, be not afraid." "Peace be unto thee"; nothing more pleasant to hear. "It is I"; nothing more pleasant to possess. "Be not afraid"; nothing safer to rejoice in. "Lo, I am with you"; nothing sweeter to enjoy.

"Always, day by day, even unto the end of the world"; nothing is surer, nothing firmer to be believed, if we would obtain life eternal.

O Lord, whatever I have, whatever I see and desire, all is nothing without Thee.

In Thee alone are all my blessings: nothing better, nothing more perfect, nothing richer, nothing more happy.

Therefore all my hope, all that I possess, all my salvation, all my peace, is in Thee, O God, my salvation: and in no created good, however beautiful, noble and great.

I say, therefore, and with the holy and humble Francis I pray: "My God and my all, I desire nothing more."

If at any time I shall be in trouble, and bereft of inward satisfaction and comfort, again I say and pray, "My God and my all, I desire nothing more." I desire nothing but Thee, my

God, all in all, and over all, and before all, blessed for ever.

O grant that I may meditate intently on these things, and ever devoutly fulfil them. Amen.

XII.—A Prayer by John Colet, Dean of St. Paul's. BORN 1466, DIED 1519.

[Dr. John Colet was a loving and lovable man, a man in advance of his age, a reformer before the Reformation, who shook off the fetters by which the intellect of men had been bound throughout the Middle Ages. By the new method of interpretation of Scripture, and the new style of preaching which he initiated, he was a benefactor to his own age; by the school which he founded—St. Paul's School—he has been a benefactor to all succeeding ages.]

We render thanks to Thee, O Almighty and everlasting God, by whose patience we have been spared, by whose power we have been upheld, and by whose bounty we have been supplied, even to this present time, and we suppliantly beseech Thee that our refreshments may be temperate, our rest moderate, our labour with care, and our wishes bounded by our wants. Thou givest liberally and upraidest not; give us the meekness of wisdom. So illuminate our dark minds with the light of Thy Divine grace, that we may know Thee, the only true God, and Jesus Christ whom Thou hast sent, whom to know is life eternal. Grant that with our whole understanding, will, and affections we may apply ourselves to obtain proficiency in practice, as well as in knowledge, thus honouring Thee who workest all in all, and without whom we can do nothing.

We pray Thee that in whatever we, day by day—whether by thought, word, or deed—offend against Thy commandments, Thou wouldst of Thy paternal favour entirely remit and frankly pardon. Let our repentance be practical, our faith active, our love unwearied, our hope patient, and our humility profound. Yet conscious of our imperfections and infirmities, may we find acceptance as we also seek forgiveness, for His sake in whom we have redemption through His blood, the forgiveness of sins according to the riches of Thy grace.

Have compassion upon our Church and nation, especially on the King's most excellent Majesty.* Be his asylum from all his enemies, his protection amidst all dangers and calamities. Make his subjects grateful, faithful and obedient. Dispense Thy Holy Spirit to all in authority, that they may consult for the public good, repress vice, recompense virtue, and advance the interests of pure and undefiled religion, that our land may be the praise of all the earth, the handmaid to piety, no less than the mistress of the arts. Banish out of the world at large all idolatry and superstition, all infidelity

* Henry the VIII.

and scepticism, all heresy and error, all tyranny and oppression, all cruelty and war, that mankind may worship Thee in the beauty of holiness. Finally, we commend to Thee this family, with all our friends, acquaintance, and neighbours. Grant us to be like-minded, one towards another, according to Christ Jesus, that we may with one mind and one mouth glorify God, even the Father of our Lord Jesus Christ. Amen.

XIII.—"A Godly Prayer." By John Knox. 1505—1572.
IN TIME OF PERSECUTION AND PERIL.

O Lord, most strong and mighty God! who destroyest the counsels of the ungodly, and at Thy pleasure riddest away the tyrants of this world, so that no force can resist Thine everlasting determination; we, Thy poor creatures and humble servants, do most earnestly desire Thee for the love Thou hast to Thy well-beloved only-begotten Son, our Lord and Saviour Jesus Christ, that Thou wilt look upon Thy cause—for it is time, O Lord!—and bring to naught all those things that are, or shall be appointed, determined and agreed against Thee and Thy holy Word. Let not the enemies of Thy truth too miserably oppress Thy Word and Thy servants which seek Thy glory: tender the advancement of

Thy pure religion, and above all things the wish in their heart that Thy holy Name alone may be glorified among all the nations. Give unto the mouth of Thy people truth and wisdom which no man may resist. And although we have most justly deserved this plague and famine of Thy Word, yet upon our true repentance, grant, we beseech Thee, that we may be thereof released. And here we promise before Thy divine Majesty better to use Thy gifts than we have done, and more straightly to order our lives according to Thy holy will and pleasure. And we will sing perpetual praises to Thy most blessed Name, world without end, through Jesus Christ our Lord.   Amen.

XIV.—Prayer of St. Francis Xavier. 1506—1552.

Thou art my God, sole object of my love;
Not for the hope of endless joys above;
Not for the fear of endless pains below,
Which they who love Thee not must undergo.

For me, and such as me, Thou deign'st to bear
An ignominious cross, the nails, the spear;
A thorny crown transpierced Thy sacred brow,
While bloody sweats from every member flow.

For me, in tortures Thou resign'dst Thy breath,
Embraced me on the Cross, and saved me by Thy death.
And can these sufferings fail my heart to move?
What but Thyself can now deserve my love!

Such as there was, and is, Thy love to me,
Such is, and shall be still, my love to Thee—
To Thee, Redeemer! mercy's sacred spring!
My God, my Father, Maker, and my King!
>—*Pope*, 1734.

XV.—A Morning Prayer. By John Calvin. 1509—1564. "Daily Offices."

["It was in the act of repeating this morning prayer of Calvin's Liturgy that the last moment of Coligny's life was spent. Early on the fatal morning of St. Bartholomew, 1572, the Admiral, who was then confined to his bed by the wound he had received from an assassin two days before, sent for his chaplain, Merlin, to engage with him in the customary devotions. While following the familiar words thus uttered, he was attacked by a band of murderers who burst into his room and dispatched him with their daggers."] C. W. Baird (New York). "A Chapter on Liturgies."

Almighty God, our Father and Preserver! We give Thee thanks that of Thy goodness Thou hast watched over us the past night and brought us to this day. We beseech Thee strengthen and guard us by Thy Spirit that we may spend it wholly in Thy service, aiming at Thy glory and the salvation of our fellow men. And even as Thou sheddest now the beams of the sun upon the earth to give light unto our bodies, so illuminate our souls with the brightness of Thy Spirit to guide us in the paths of Thine obedience. May all our purpose be this day to honour and serve Thee; may we look for all prosperity to Thy blessing only, and seek no object but such as may be pleasing in Thy sight. Enable us, O Lord, while we labour for the body and the life that now is, ever to look beyond unto that heavenly life which Thou hast promised Thy children. Defend us in soul and body from all harm. Guard us against all assaults of the devil, and deliver us from any danger that may beset us. And seeing it is a small thing to have begun well except we also persevere, take us, O Lord, into Thy good keeping this day and all our days. Continue and increase Thy grace within us, until we shall be perfectly united in the glory of Thy Son Jesus Christ our Lord, the Sun of Righteousness, who shall replenish our souls with His eternal light and gladness. And that we may obtain all these mercies be pleased to cast out of Thy remembrance all our past offences, and of Thy boundless mercy forgive them, as Thou hast promised those who call upon Thee in sincerity and truth. Hear us, O God our Father and Redeemer, through Jesus Christ our Lord. In whose name we pray, as He hath taught us, Our Father, &c. Amen.

XVI.—An Evening Prayer. By John Calvin. 1509—1564.

["As well for the happiness of the language as for the beauty of the leading thoughts in which the suggestions of night and darkness are treated with exquisite feeling, we have long considered this prayer the

finest composition of the kind that has fallen under our notice. . . ."
"It was in the language of this prayer that the illustrious Reformer, John Knox, breathed his dying thoughts to God."] C. W. Baird (New York). "A Chapter on Liturgies," p. 64.

O Merciful God! Eternal Light, shining in darkness, Thou who dispellest the night of sin and all blindness of heart, since Thou hast appointed the night for rest and the day for labour, we beseech Thee grant that our bodies may rest in peace and quietness, that afterward they may be able to endure the labour they must bear. Temper our sleep that it be not disorderly, that we may remain spotless both in body and soul, yea that our sleep itself may be to Thy glory. Enlighten the eyes of our understanding that we may not sleep in death, but always look for deliverance from this misery. Defend us against all assaults of the devil and take us into Thy holy protection. And although we have not passed this day without greatly sinning against Thee, we beseech Thee to hide our sins with Thy mercy, as Thou hidest all things on earth with the darkness of the night, that we may not be cast out from Thy presence. Relieve and comfort all those who are afflicted in mind, body, or estate. Through Jesus Christ our Lord, who hath taught us to pray, "Our Father, &c." Amen.

XVII.—**Another Prayer by John Calvin (Liturgy of Geneva).**
  1509—1564. REPRODUCED IN THE REFORMED DUTCH LITURGY. BEFORE COMMUNION.

Most Gracious God we beseech Thee that as Thy Son hath not only once offered up His Body and Blood upon the Cross for the remission of our sins, but hath also vouchsafed them unto us for our meat and drink unto eternal life, so Thou wilt grant us grace, with sincere hearts and fervent desires, to accept this great blessing at His hands. May we by lively faith partake of His Body and Blood, yea, of Himself, true God and Man, the only bread from Heaven which giveth life unto our souls. Suffer us no longer to live unto ourselves according to a corrupt and sinful nature; but may He live in us, and lead us to the life that is holy, blessed, and unchangeable for ever. Thus make us true partakers of the new and everlasting testament which is the covenant of grace. And thus assure us of Thy willingness ever to be our gracious Father; not imputing unto us our sins, but that we may magnify Thy name in our words and works, providing us as Thy beloved children and heirs with all things necessary for our good. Fit us, O Heavenly Father, so to celebrate at this time the blessed remembrance of Thy beloved Son. Enable us profitably to contemplate His love and show forth the benefits of His death; that, receiving fresh increase of strength in Thy faith and in all good works, we may with greater confidence call Thee our Father, and evermore rejoice in Thee, through Jesus Christ our Redeemer. Amen.

XVIII.—Prayer by John Calvin (Liturgy of Geneva). 1509—1564. CONFESSION.

[This prayer is to be traced in all the Reformed Liturgies, and even in the Anglican Prayer Book.]

Lord God, Eternal and Almighty Father! We acknowledge and confess before Thy holy majesty, that we are poor sinners, conceived and born in guilt and in corruption; prone to do evil, unable of ourselves to do any good; who, by reason of our depravity, transgress without end Thy holy commandments. Therefore we have drawn upon ourselves by Thy just sentence, condemnation and death. But, O Lord, with heartfelt sorrow we repent and deplore our offences! We condemn ourselves and our evil ways; with true penitence beseeching that Thy grace may relieve our distress.

Be pleased then to have compassion upon us, O most gracious God, Father of all mercies, for the sake of Thy Son Jesus Christ our Lord. And in removing our guilt and our pollution, grant us the daily increase of the grace of Thine Holy Spirit, that, acknowledging from our inmost hearts our own unrighteousness, we may be touched with sorrow that shall work true repentance, and that Thy Spirit, mortifying all sins within us, may produce the fruits of holiness and of righteousness well pleasing in Thy sight, through Jesus Christ our Lord. Amen.

XIX.—Prayer of Martin Luther on the morning of the 18th of April, 1521, the day when he was brought before the Diet at Worms.

"His faith grew weak; his enemies multiplied before him; his imagination was overwhelmed at the sight. . . . In this hour of bitter sorrow, in which he drinks the cup of Christ, and which was to him a Garden of Gethsemane, he falls to the earth and utters these broken cries which we cannot understand unless we can figure to ourselves the depth of the anguish whence they ascend to God";—

"O Almighty and everlasting God! How terrible is this world! Behold it openeth its mouth to swallow me up, and I have so little trust in Thee! How weak is the flesh and how powerful is Satan! If it is in the strength of this world only that I must put my trust, all is over! My last hour is come, my condemnation has been pronounced. O God!

O God! O God! do Thou help me against all the wisdom of the world! Do this; Thou shouldst do this; Thou alone, for this is not my work but Thine! *I* have nothing to do here, nothing to contend for with these great ones of the world! I should desire to see my days flow on peaceful and happy. But the cause is Thine, and it is a righteous and eternal cause. O Lord! help me! Faithful and unchangeable God! In no man do I place my trust. It would be vain—all that is of man is uncertain, all that cometh of man fails. O God! My God, hearest Thou me not? My God art Thou dead? No! no, Thou can'st not die! Thou hidest Thyself only! Thou hast chosen me for this work. I know it well! Act, then, O God, stand at my side, for the sake of Thy well-beloved Son Jesus Christ, who is my defence, my shield, and my strong tower."

After a moment of silent struggle, he thus continued :—

"Lord! where stayest Thou! O my God where art Thou? Come! Come! I am ready! I am ready to lay down my life for Thy truth, patient as a lamb. For it is the cause of justice—it is Thine! I will never separate myself from Thee, neither now nor through eternity! And though the world may be filled with devils, though my body, which is still the work of Thy hands, should be slain, be stretched upon the pavement, be cut in pieces, reduced to ashes—my soul is Thine! Yes! I have the assurance of Thy word. My soul belongs to Thee! It shall abide for ever with Thee. Amen. O God! help me. Amen.

"This prayer explains Luther and the Reformation. History here raises the veil of the sanctuary, and discloses to our view the secret place whence strength and courage were imparted to this humble and despised man who was the instrument of God to emancipate the soul and the thoughts of men, and to open a new era. . . . In our opinion it is one of the most precious documents in all history."

HISTORY OF THE REFORMATION.
By Merle D'Aubigné.

[It was in the evening of that same day that Luther, standing in the midst of the great assembly, uttered those memorable words: "I cannot and I will not retract. Here I stand, I can do no other. May God help me! Amen."—ED.]

XX.—Prayer of the Lady Vittoria Colonna, Marchioness of Pescara. A follower of Juan Valdez, one of the Heroes of the Reformation in Italy. 1541.

Thanks to Thy sovereign grace O God, if I
    Am graft in that true Vine a living shoot,
    Whose arms embrace the world, and in whose root
Planted by faith, our life must hidden lie.
But Thou beholdest how I fade and dry
    Choked with a waste of leaf and void of fruit
    Unless Thy spring perennial shall recruit
My sapless branch, still waiting fresh supply.

> O, cleanse me, then, and make me to abide
> > Wholly in Thee, to drink Thy heavenly dew,
> > And watered daily with my tears, to grow.
> Thou art the Truth, Thy promise is my guide;
> > Prepare me when Thou comest, Lord, to show
> > Fruits answering to the stock on which I grow.

XXI.—**Another Prayer by Vittoria Colonna.** 1543. [For Renewal of Spiritual Life.]

Grant, I pray, O Lord, that with that lowliness of mind which befits my humble condition, and that elevation of soul which Thy majesty demands, I may ever adore Thee; may I continually live in that fear which Thy justice inspires, in that hope which Thy clemency permits. May I submit myself to Thee as All-powerful, leave myself in Thy hands as All-wise, and turn unto Thee as All-perfect and good. I beseech Thee, most merciful Father, that Thy most vivid fire may purify me; that Thy clearest light may illuminate me, and that purest love of Thine may so advance me that, held back by no mortal influence, I may return safe and happy to Thee.

XXII.—**A Hymn of Prayer.** Attributed to **Sir Walter Raleigh.** 1552—1618.

> Rise, oh my soul, with thy desires to heaven:
> > And with devoutest contemplation use
> > Thy time, where time's eternity is given;

      And let vain thoughts no more thy thoughts abuse,
        But down in darkness let them lie ;
        So live thy better, let thy worse thoughts die !

And thou my soul, inspired with holy flame,
    View and review, with most regardful eye
That Holy Cross, whence thy salvation came,
    On which thy Saviour and thy sin did die !
        For in that sacred object is much pleasure,
        And in that Saviour is my life, my treasure !

To Thee, O Jesus, I direct my eyes,
    To Thee my hands, to Thee my humble knees,
To Thee my heart shall offer sacrifice ;
    To Thee my thoughts, who my thoughts only sees—
        To Thee myself ; myself and all I give ;
        To Thee I die ; to Thee I only live !

XXIII.—**A Prayer on Awaking. By Lancelot Andrewes, Bishop of Winchester. From "Private Devotions."** 1555—1626.

Blessed art Thou, O Lord
                Our God
        The God of our Fathers ;
Who turnest the shadow of death into the morning,
    and renewest the face of the earth :
Who rollest away the darkness from before the light,
    banishest night, and bringest back the day ;
Who lightenest mine eyes
        lest I sleep the sleep of death ;
Who deliverest me from the terror by night,
    from the pestilence that walketh in darkness :
Who drivest sleep from mine eyes
        and slumber from mine eyelids ;

Who makest the outgoings of the morning
>   and evening to rejoice;
>   because I laid me down and slept and awaked
>   for the Lord sustained me;
>   because I waked and beheld
>   and my sleep was sweet unto me.
Blot out as a thick cloud of night my transgressions
>   and scatter as a morning cloud my sins.
Grant me to be a child of the light and of the day,
>   to walk soberly, spotlessly, honestly as in the day.
Vouchsafe to keep me this day without sin.
Thou who upholdest the falling and liftest the fallen,
>   let me not harden my heart in provocation
>   or temptation, or deceitfulness of sin;
Moreover deliver me this day
>   from the snare of the fowler
>   and from the noisome pestilence,
>   from the arrow that flieth by day
>   from the destruction that wasteth at noonday.
Defend this day against my evil
>   against the evil of this day defend Thou me.
Let not my days be spent in vanity
>   nor my years in sorrow.
>   Day unto day uttereth speech:
>   to-day some knowledge, or deed, unto yesterday;
Cause me to hear Thy loving kindness in the morning
>   for in Thee do I trust;
Cause me to know the way wherein I should walk
>   for I lift up my soul unto Thee.
Deliver me, O Lord, from mine enemies;
>   I flee unto Thee to hide me.
Teach me to do Thy will
>   for Thou art my God;
>   Thy Spirit is good,
>   lead me into the land of uprightness.

Quicken me, O Lord, for Thy name's sake,
    for Thy righteousness sake,
      bring my soul out of trouble.
Remove from me foolish imaginations,
      inspire those which are good
      and pleasing in Thy sight.
Turn away mine eyes
      from beholding vanity;
    let mine eyes look right on
And let mine eyelids look straight before me.
Hedge up mine enemies with thorns
      lest they incline to undisciplined words.
Give me early the ear to hear
  and open mine eyes to the instruction of Thine oracles.
Set a watch, O Lord, before my mouth,
      Keep the door of my lips.
Let my speech be seasoned with salt
    That it may minister grace to the hearers.
Let no deed be grief unto me
        nor offence of heart;
Let me do some work
   for which Thou wilt remember me, Lord, for good,
   and spare me according to the multitude of Thy mercies.
Into Thy hands I commit
      my spirit, soul, and body
    which Thou hast created, redeemed, regenerated
      O Lord, Thou God of Truth!
      and together with me
  all mine, and all that belongs to me!
     Lord in Thy goodness
    preserve us from all evil
      preserve our souls.
    I beseech Thee O Lord
      Keep us from falling

and present us faultless
in the presence of Thy glory
in that day.
Preserve my going out and my coming in
from this time forth and even for evermore.
Prosper, I pray Thee, Thy servant this day
and grant him mercy
in the sight of those who meet him.
O God make speed to save me!
O Lord make haste to help me!
O turn unto me
and have mercy upon me.
Give Thy strength unto Thy servant
and save the son of Thy handmaid.
Show me a token for good,
that they who hate me may see it and be ashamed:
because, Thou, Lord, hast holpen me
and comforted me.

[Dr. Whyte* says: "Every page, almost every line of the *Private Devotions* has some strong word in it, some startling word, some selected, compounded and compacted word, some heart-laden clause, some scriptural or liturgical expression set in a blaze of new light and life, and ever after to be filled with new power as we employ it in our prayers and praises."]

XXIV.—An Evening Prayer for Grace. By Lancelot Andrewes, Bishop of Winchester. 1555—1626.

Having spent the day
I give Thee thanks, O Lord.
Evening draws nigh,
make it bright.

* Quoted from "Lancelot Andrewes and his Private Devotions." By Dr. Alex. Whyte. Nisbet & Co., Limited.

As day has its evening
so also has life.
The evening of life is age;
Age has overtaken me;
make it bright.
Cast me not off in the time of old age
forsake me not when my strength faileth.
Even to my old age be Thou He
and even to hoar hairs carry me
do Thou make, do Thou bear,
do Thou carry and deliver me.
Abide with me Lord
for it is toward evening
and the day is far spent
of this toilful life;
Let Thy strength be made perfect
in my weakness.

The day is fled and gone;
life, too, is going
This lifeless life.
Night cometh,
and cometh death;
The deathless death.
As the end of the day is near
so too is the end of life;
We then, also remembering it,
beseech of Thee
for the close of our life
that Thou wouldest guide it in peace
to be Christian, acceptable, sinless, shameless,
and, if it please Thee, painless.
Lord, O Lord, gathering us together
under the feet of Thy chosen,

whom Thou wilt and as Thou wilt
only without shame and sin.
Let us remember the days of darkness
for they are many
lest we be cast into outer darkness.
Let us remember to outstrip the night
doing some good thing.
Near is judgment;
A good and acceptable answer
at the dread and awful judgment seat
of Jesus Christ
Vouchsafe to us, O Lord!*

XXV.—**A Prayer to my God in a night of my late Sickness. By Sir Henry Wotton. 1568—1639.**

O Thou great power! in whom we move,
　By whom we live, in whom we die,
Behold me through Thy beams of love
　While on this couch of tears I lie;
And cleanse my sordid soul within
　By Thy Christ's blood, the bath of sin.

No hallowed oils, no gums I need,
　No rags of saints, no purging fire;
One rosy drop from David's seed
　Was worlds of seas to quench Thine ire.
O precious Ransom! which, once paid,
That *consummatum est* was said;

And said by Him who said no more,
　But sealed it with His sacred breath;

---

* Quoted from "Lancelot Andrewes and his Private Devotions." By Dr. Alex. Whyte. Nisbet & Co., Limited.

> Thou then that hath disponged my score
> And, dying, wert the death of Death,
> Be to me now,—on Thee I call,—
> My Life, my Strength, my Joy, my All.

XXVI.—A Prayer by Archbishop Laud. Born 1573, beheaded 1645.

O Lord and most merciful Father, against heaven and in Thy sight have we sinned; blot out, we beseech Thee, all our sins from the book of Thy remembrance which Thou hast written before Thee: give us henceforth wise and sober, believing, penitent, and obedient hearts—souls full of devotion to do Thee service; and grant us evermore strength against all temptations.

O blessed Lord, enable us to fulfil Thy commands, and command what Thou wilt. Prepare our souls for Thy coming and come when Thou wilt, O Thou Saviour of all who hope in Thee. Do with us and ours as shall seem best in Thine own eyes; only vouchsafe us patient and dependent spirits. Make our service acceptable unto Thee while we live, and our souls ready for Thee when we die. Give us grace in this life and glory in the life to come.

Bless O gracious Father, Thine holy Catholic Church. Fill it with truth and grace. Where it is corrupt, purge it; where it is in error, direct it;

where it is superstitious, rectify it; where it is amiss, reform it; where it is right, strengthen and confirm it; where it is divided and rent asunder, heal the breaches of it, O Thou Holy One of Israel. Bless all those who are called to any office or ministration in Thy Church; replenish them with the truth of Thy doctrine, and with integrity and innocence of life; remember all their offerings and accept their burnt sacrifice. O Lord, let their prayers be precious in Thine ears, and the cries of all Thy people, even of the city of God, be not in vain.

Almighty God, bless and preserve our King, and all in authority under him. Comfort all that are in affliction. Give Thy blessing to all our relations and friends, to every member of this family whether present or absent: and grant us grace to forgive our enemies, if we have any, as we trust to be ourselves forgiven, through the merits and mediation of Jesus Christ who, with Thee O Father and with Thee O Holy Spirit, liveth and reigneth one God, world without end. Amen.

XXVII.—A Prayer by Ben Jonson, to the Holy Trinity.
    1574—1637.

    O Holy, blessed, glorious Trinitie
    Of Persons, still one God in Unitie,
    The faithful man's beleevéd mysterie,
            Helpe, helpe to lift

Myselfe up to Thee, harrow'd, torne, and bruised
By sinne and Sathan and my flesh misused;
As my heart lies in peeces, all confused,
    O take my gift.

All-gracious God, the sinner's sacrifice,
A broken heart Thou wert not wont despise;
But 'bove the fat of rammes and bulls, to prize—
    An offering meet
For Thy acceptance; O behold me right
And take compassion on my grievous plight!
What odour can be than a heart contrite
    To Thee more sweet?

Eternall Father, God, who didst create
This All of nothing, gav'st it form and fate
And breath'd into it life and light and state,
    To worship Thee!
Eternall God, the Sonne, who not denyd'st
To take our nature; becam'st man, and died'st
To pay our debts, upon Thy Crosse, and cryd'st
    All's done in Me!

Eternall Spirit, God from both proceeding,
Father and Sonne—the Comforter, imbreeding
Pure thoughts in man, with fiery zeale them feeding
    For acts of grace!
Increase those acts, O Glorious Unitie,
Of Persons, still one God in Trinitie
Till I attain the longed-for mysterie
    Of seeing your face,

Beholding One in Three, and Three in One,
A Trinitie to shine in Union;
The gladdest light darke man can thinke upon—
    O grant it me!

Father, and Sonne and Holy Ghost, you Three,
All co-eternall in your Majestie
Distinct in Persons, yet in Unitie—
           One God to see.

My Maker, Saviour and my Sanctifier!
To heare, to meditate, to sweeten my desire
With grace and love, with cherishing entire;
           Oh then how blest!
Among Thy saints elected to abide,
And with Thy angels placéd side by side,
But in Thy presence truly glorified,
           Shall I there rest.

        From "The Underwoods" (Poems of Devotion).

XXVIII.—Prayer by Bishop Hall. 1574—1656.

O my God, I am justly ashamed to think what favours I have received from Thee, and what poor returns I have made to Thee. Truly, Lord, I must needs say Thou hast thought nothing either in earth or in heaven too good for me; and I, on the other side, have grudged Thee that weak and worthless obedience which Thou hast required of me. Alas! what pleasure could I have done to Thee who art infinite, if I had sacrificed my whole self to Thee, as Thou commandest? Thou art, and wilt be, Thyself, though the world were not; it is I, I only, that could be a gainer by this happy match, which to my own wrong I have unthankfully neglected. I see it is not so much what we have as how we employ it. Oh Thou that hast been so bountiful in heaping Thy rich mercies upon me, vouchsafe to grant me yet one gift more; give me grace and power to improve all Thy gifts to the glory of the Giver, otherwise it had been better for me to have been poor than ungrateful.

[Warton, in his "History of Poetry," says of the writings of Bishop Hall:—"His chief fault is obscurity, arising from a remote phraseology, constrained combinations, unfamiliar allusions, elliptical apostrophes, and abruptness of expression."]

XXIX.—A Prayer of Contrition. By Jacob Böhme. 1575—1624.

[Jacob Böhme (or Behmen) was the son of a peasant at Görlitz in Silesia, where he lived as a shoemaker, and the author of many works on philosophy and religion.]

"Behmen is so deep and so original in his purely philosophical, theological, and speculative books, that in many places we can only stand back and wonder at the man. But in his *Holy Week*, Behmen kneels down beside us. Not but that his characteristic depth is present in his prayers also; but we all know something of the nature, the manner, and the blessedness of prayer, and thus it is that we are so much more at home with Behmen the prodigal son, than we are with Behmen the theosophical theologian. When Behmen begins to teach us to pray, and when the lesson comes to us out of his own closet, then we are able to see in a nearer light something of the originality, the greatness, the strength, and the true and genuine piety of the philosopher and the theologian. When Behmen's philosophy and theology become penitence, prayer, and praise, then by their fruits we know how good his philosophy and his theology must be, away down in their deepest and most hidden nature."

JACOB BEHMEN, *An Appreciation,*
By Alex. Whyte, D.D.

O Thou mighty, unsearchable, and holy God, Lord of all beings, who of Thy great love to us, hast in Jesus Christ revealed Thy holy essence in our humanity; I am a sinful man come before Thy face, though I am not worthy to lift up my eyes to Thee. I confess that I have been unfaithful to Thy love and grace, and have broken the covenant which Thou hast made with me in my baptism when Thou didst accept me as Thy child and an inheritor of eternal life. Thee have I forsaken and turned my desires to the vanities of this world and contaminated my soul with them. I am yet sunk in the sins and vanity of my corrupt flesh, and have but one little spark of the living breath of Thy spirit in me which longs for Thy grace. I am faint and powerless; I am a wild branch in Thy vine; I have squandered my portion in the evil pleasures of this world. O God in Christ Jesus, who didst become man for the sake of poor sinners that Thou mightest succour them, unto Thee do I haste, unto Thee I lament my need, unto Thee do I cry for aid, for

Thou art my only refuge, and there is yet a little spark of faith and trust in Thee left alive in my soul. Here I stand, poor and destitute before Thee. I cast me at Thy feet. I call upon Thy compassion. Accept me, O Lord, in Thy death and let my sinful life perish therein. Smite down my selfishness; slay, through Thy death, this self-love in me that I may no longer live to myself but unto Thee who hast died for me. O Thou rich Fountain of the Love of God, let me be buried in my Saviour's death to my vain ambitions and my sins. O Thou Breath of the mighty Love of God, fan the dim spark of Thy spirit within me, that I may begin to hunger and thirst after Thee! Oh how powerless is my soul! Give Thou her to drink from Thy sweet fountain of living waters, that she may be awakened from her deathly lethargy. Convert Thou me, O Lord, for I cannot convert myself. Thou Conqueror over death, help me in my strife and redeem me from the fetters of Satan. Vanquish my self-love, melt my stubborn will, break my hard heart, that I may live in Thy fear and be obedient as an instrument in Thy hands, willing only what Thou wilt. O Thou Abyss of Love draw the desires of my soul unto Thyself, and lead me out of death into Thy resurrection.

O God the Holy Spirit in Christ my Saviour, teach me what I should do to turn unto Thee; convert Thou my will, draw me, through Christ, to the Father, help me to depart from all sin and vanity, and never again to consent thereto voluntarily. Awake in me true repentance for my sins past. Keep me in Thy cords, and never let me go away from Thee lest the enemy once more lead me back through my own weak, evil, flesh and blood into the state of death.

Yes: Thou faithful God: in myself I am blind and know not myself for vanity; even Thou art hidden from me, Who art yet so close to me. O suffer a ray of Thy grace to reach my soul. I lie before Thee like a dying man, whose life is just hovering on his lips. Quicken me, O Lord, and raise me up as a living soul. I wait upon Thy promise who hast said: "As I live I have no pleasure in the death of a sinner but that he should be converted and live." Now, therefore, I sink into the death of my Redeemer and wait for Thee: Thy Word is Life and Truth. Amen.

XXX.—A Litany to the Holy Spirit. By Robert Herrick. 1591—1674.

[There were great incongruities in the life as in the writings of Robert Herrick. His poems were of two kinds, love songs—often indecent—and sacred pieces, but both "exhibiting a richness of fancy mingled with the quaintness of the age in which he lived such as to render him worthy of a high place in the scale of British lyrical poets." "When the ore is pure," says Campbell, "it is of great value."—Ed.]

Robert Herrick. 1591.

In the hour of my distress,
When temptations me oppress,
And when I my sins confess,
   Sweet Spirit, comfort me!

When I lie within my bed,
Sick in heart and sick in head,
And with doubts discomfited,
   Sweet Spirit, comfort me!

When the house doth sigh and weep,
And the world is drowned in sleep,
Yet mine eyes the watch do keep,
   Sweet Spirit, comfort me!

When the artless doctor sees
No one hope but of his fees,
And his skill runs on the lees,
   Sweet Spirit, comfort me!

When the passing-bell doth toll,
And the furies in a shoal
Come to fright a parting soul,
   Sweet Spirit, comfort me!

When the tapers now burn blue,
And the comforters are few,
And that number more than true,
   Sweet Spirit, comfort me!

When the priest his last has prayed,
And I nod to what is said
'Cause my speech is now decayed,
   Sweet Spirit, comfort me!

When, God knows, I'm tossed about,
Either with despair, or doubt;
Yet before the glass be out,
    Sweet Spirit, comfort me!

When the tempter me pursu'th
With the sins of all my youth,
And half damns me with untruth,
    Sweet Spirit, comfort me!

When the flames and hellish cries
Fright mine ears and fright mine eyes,
And all terrors me surprise,
    Sweet Spirit, comfort me!

When the judgment is revealed,
And that opened which was sealed,
When to Thee I have appealed,
    Sweet Spirit, comfort me!

XXXI.—A Prayer by George Herbert, "the Sweetest Singer of the English Church." 1593—1632. Entitled "The Elixir."

Teach me, my God and King,
  In all things Thee to see,
And what I do in anything,
  To do it as for Thee.

A man that looks on glass,
  On it may stay his eye,
Or if he pleaseth through it pass,
  And then the heaven espy.

All may of Thee partake ;
  Nothing can be so mean
Which with this tincture (for Thy sake)
  Will not grow bright and clean.

A servant with this clause
  Makes drudgery divine ;
Who sweeps a room, as for Thy laws,
  Makes that and the action fine.

This is the famous stone
  That turneth all to Gold ;
For that which God doth touch and own
  Cannot for less be told.

XXXII.—A Prayer composed by Queen Elizabeth in 1597.

["Her entire nature was saturated with artifice. Except when speaking some round untruth Elizabeth never could be simple. Her letters and her speeches were as fantastic as her dress, and her meaning as involved as her policy. She was unnatural even in her prayers, and she carried her affectations into the presence of the Almighty."—Froude's "History of England," vol. xii., p. 507.]

Oh, God, Almaker, Keeper, and Guider, inurement of Thy rare seen and seeld heard of goodness, poured in so plentiful a sort upon us full oft, breeds now this boldness to crave with bowed knees and hearts of humility Thy large hand of helping power, to assist with wonder our just cause, not founded on prides' motion or begun on malice stock, but, as Thou best knowest, to whom nought is hid, grounded on just defence from wrongs, hate, and bloody desire of conquest, for since means Thou hast imparted to save, that Thou hast given by enjoying* such a people as scorns their bloodshed, where surely ours is one. Fortify, dear God, such hearts in such sort as their best part may be worst, that to the truest part meant worse with least loss to such a nation as despise their lives for their country's good; that all foreign lands may laud and admire the omnipotency of Thy works, a fact alone for Thee only to perform. So shall Thy name be spread for wonders wrought, and the faithful encouraged to repose in Thy unfellowed grace; and we that minded naught but right enchained in Thy bonds for perpetual slavery, and live and die the sacrificers of our souls for such obtained favours. Warrant, dear Lord, all this with Thy command.

Strype, "Annals," vol. iv., p. 440.

XXXIII.—A Family Prayer by King Charles I. BORN 1600, BEHEADED 30TH JANUARY, 1649.

["The death of Charles gave fresh vigour to the royalist cause; and the loyalty which it revived was stirred to enthusiasm by the publication of the 'Eikon Basilike,' a work really due to the ingenuity of Dr. Gauden, a Presbyterian Minister, but which was believed to have been composed by the King himself in his later hours of captivity, and which reflected with admirable skill, the hopes, the suffering, and the piety of the royal 'martyr.'"—Green's "History of the English People," vol. iii., p. 265.]

To Thee, O our God, do we direct our prayers, who alone canst enlighten our darkness and quicken

---

* *Sic* in Strype, (?) "employing."

our dulness. Nothing, O Lord, is to Thee so great that it may resist Thee; nor anything so little that it may be despised by Thee. Look upon our misery with the eyes of Thy mercy, and let Thine Almighty power work deliverance for us. Let not Satan, we beseech Thee, triumph over us, nor the world be ministers of Thy justice, but our sins, by Thine own hands, be punished.

In Thee, O blessed Jesus, is all fulness; from Thee all sufficiency, by Thee all acceptance. Thou art our King; reign over us and in us. Thou art our prophet, teach us. Thou art our priest: pray not only for us, but in us. Unworthy though we are, yet Thou breakest not the bruised reed, nor quenchest the smoking flax till Thou bring forth judgment unto victory and truth. Let Thy tenderness touch us, Thy love heal our backslidings, Thy goodness lead us to repentance, Thy power make strong our faith, Thy Spirit help our infirmities.

Abase, O Lord God, the pride of all our hearts, that we may humble ourselves under Thy mighty hand, and that Thou mayst exalt us in due time. Only thus much let us beg of Thee—and let our beseeching, O Lord, be accepted of Thee, since it even proceeds from Thyself—that by Thy goodness Thou wilt suffer some beam of Thy Majesty so to shine in our minds that we who, in our greatest affliction, acknowledge it our noblest title to be Thy creatures, may still depend confidently on Thee as Thy saints and servants, even as Thy dear children. Let calamity be the exercise, but not the overthrow of our virtue. O let not any prevailing power be to our destruction. If it be Thy will that we should be tried for our punishment, never, O Lord, let wickedness gain the ascendancy, but grant that we may still maintain a pure mind and steadfast resolution to serve Thee, without fear or presumption, yet with that humble assurance which may best please Thee, so that, at the last we may come to Thy eternal Kingdom, through the merits of Thy Son, our only Saviour, Jesus Christ. Amen.

XXXIV.—Prayers. By Jeremy Taylor, D.D., Chaplain in Ordinary to King Charles I. BORN 1613, DIED 1667.

[The nightly prayer of Bishop Jeremy Taylor was, for himself and his friends, God's merciful deliverance and preservation from :—

"The violence and rule of passion, from a servile will, and a commanding lust; from pride and vanity; from false opinion and ignorant confidence;

"From improvidence and prodigality; from envy and the spirit of slander; from sensuality; from presumption and from despair;

"From a state of temptation and a hardened spirit; from delaying of repentance and persevering in sin; from unthankfulness and irreligion; and from seducing others;

"From all infatuation of soul, folly, and madness; from wilfulness, self-love, and vain ambition; from a vicious life and an unprovided death."]

A Prayer for the Graces of Faith, Hope, and Charity.

O Lord God of infinite mercy, of infinite excellency, who hast sent Thy Holy Son into the world to redeem us from an intolerable misery, and to teach us a holy religion, and to forgive us our infinite debt: give me Thy Holy Spirit, that my understanding and all my faculties may be so resigned to the discipline and doctrine of my Lord that I may be prepared in mind and will to die for the testimony of Jesus, and to suffer any affliction or calamity that shall offer to hinder my duty, or tempt me to shame, or sin, or apostacy: and let my faith be the parent of a good life, a strong shield to repel the fiery darts of the devil, and the author of a holy hope, of modest desires, of confidence in God, and of a never-failing charity to Thee, my God, and to all the world; that I may never have my portion with the unbelievers or uncharitable and desperate persons: but may be supported by the strengths of faith in all temptations, and may be refreshed with the comforts of a holy hope in all my sorrows, and may bear the burden of the Lord and the infirmities of my neighbour, by the support of charity: that the yoke of Jesus may become easy to me, and my love may do all the miracles of grace, till, from grace it swell to glory, from earth to heaven, from duty to reward, from the imperfections of a beginning and still growing love, it may arrive at the consummation of an eternal and never-ceasing charity, through Jesus Christ the Son of Thy love, the anchor of our hope, the author and finisher of our faith, to whom with Thee, O Lord God, Father of heaven and earth, and with Thy Holy Spirit be all glory and love and obedience and dominion now and for ever.   Amen.

From " Holy Living and Dying."

XXXV.—Another Prayer by Jeremy Taylor. 1613—1667.

O most glorious and powerful Jesus, who with Thine own right hand and Thy holy arm hath gotten to Thyself, on our behalf, the victory over sin, hell, and the grave ; remember this Thy mercy and truth, which Thou hast promised to all that believe in Thee ; give us pardon of our sins, sealed unto us by the testimony of thy Holy Spirit and of a good conscience ; and grant that we, by Thy strength, may fight against our ghostly enemies and by Thy power may overcome them, that we may rejoice in a holy peace and sing and give Thee thanks for our victory and our crown. Extend this mercy, and enlarge the effect of Thy great victories to the heathen, that all the ends of the earth may sing a new song unto Thee, and see the salvation of God: that, when Thou comest to judge the earth, we may all find mercy, and be joyful together before Thee in the festivity of a blessed eternity, through Thy mercies, O blessed Saviour and Redeemer, Jesus. Amen.

XXXVI.—A Prayer by Drummond of Hawthornden. 1617.

A Prayer.

Great God, whom we with humble thoughts adore,
Eternal, Infinite, Almighty King,
Whose palace heaven transcends, whose throne before
Archangels serve and Seraphim do sing ;
Of nought who wrought all that with wondering eyes
We do behold within this spacious round ;
Who mak'st the rocks to rock, and stand the skies ;
At whose command the horrid thunders sound ;
Ah ! spare us worms ; weigh not how we, alas !
Evil to ourselves, against Thy laws rebel ;
Wash off those spots which still in conscience' glass,
Though we be loth to look, we see too well.
Deserved revenge O do not, do not take.
If Thou revenge, what shall abide Thy blow ?
Pass shall this world, this world which Thou didst make,
Which should not perish till Thy trumpet blow.
For who is he whom parents' sin not stains,
Or with his own offence is not defiled ?
Though Justice ruin threaten, Justice' reins
Let Mercy hold, and be both just and mild.

From "Spiritual Poems." Quoted in "Drummond of Hawthornden ; The Story of his Life and Writings." By David Masson, M.A., LL.D., p. 65.

XXXVII.—A General Prayer. From Baxter's Reformed Liturgy. 1615—1691.

[The whole Liturgy was drawn up by Richard Baxter in a fortnight, "nor could he make use of any book except a Bible and a Concordance; but he compared it all with the Assembly's Directory and the Book of Common Prayer."—Orme's "Life of Baxter," p. 407.]

O most holy, blessed and glorious Trinity, Father, Son, and Holy Ghost, Three persons and one God, our Creater, Redeemer, and Sanctifier, our Lord, our Governor and Father, hear us and have mercy upon us, miserable sinners.

O Lord our Saviour, God and man! who, having assumed our nature by Thy sufferings and death and burial, wast made a ransom to take away the sins of the world; who, being raised from the dead, ascended and glorified, art made Head over all things to the Church which Thou gatherest, justifiest, sanctifiest, rulest and preservest, and which, at Thy coming, Thou wilt raise and judge to endless glory: we beseech Thee to hear us, miserable sinners.

Make sure to us our calling and election, our unfeigned faith and repentance, that being justified and made the sons of God we may have peace with Him as our reconciled God and Father.

Let Thy Holy Spirit sanctify us and dwell in us, and cause us to deny ourselves, and to give up ourselves entirely to Thee, as being not our own but Thine.

As the world was created for Thy glory, let Thy name be glorified throughout the world; let self-love and pride and vain glory be destroyed; cause us to love Thee, fear Thee, and trust in Thee with all our hearts, and to live to Thee.

Let all the earth subject themselves to Thee, their King. Let the kingdoms of the world become the kingdom of the Lord and of His Christ. Let the atheists, idolators, Mahometans, Jews, and other infidels and ungodly people be converted. Send forth meet labourers into the harvest and let the gospel be preached throughout all the world. Preserve and bless them in Thy work. Sustain in patience and seasonably deliver the churches that are oppressed by idolators, infidels, Mahometans or other enemies, or by the Roman papal ursurpations.

Unite all Christians in Jesus Christ, the true and only universal Head, in the true Christian and Catholic faith and love; cast out heresies and corruptions; heal divisions; let the strong receive the weak and bear their infirmities; restrain the spirit of pride and cruelty and let nothing be done in strife or vain glory.

Keep us from atheism, idolatry and rebellion against Thee; from infidelity, ungodliness and sensuality; from security and presumption and despair. Let us delight to please Thee, and let Thy Word be the rule of our faith and lives; let us love it and understand it, and meditate in it day and night.

Let us not corrupt or neglect Thy worship; nor take Thy holy name in vain. Keep us from blasphemy, perjury, profane swearing, lying, contempt of Thy ordinances, and from false, unworthy and unreverent thoughts and speeches of God or holy things, and from the neglect and profanation of Thy holy day. . . .

[Here follow petitions for Kings and Rulers, especially "Thy servant Charles our King," and also for pastors and teachers, for parents, and for strength to keep the several items of the moral law as set forth in the Ten Commandments. The general prayer concludes thus:]

Cause us to watch against temptations, to resist and overcome the flesh, the devil and the world, and by no allurements of pleasure, profit or honour to be drawn from Thee to sin; let us patiently suffer with Christ that we may rejoice with Him.

Deliver us and all Thy people from the enmity and rage of Satan and all his wicked instruments, and preserve us to Thy heavenly kingdom.

For Thou art the universal King: all power is

Thine in heaven and earth; of Thee, and through Thee, and to Thee, are all things, and the glory shall be Thine for ever. Amen.

XXXVIII.—A Prayer of Blaise Pascal, in Time of Sickness. 1623—1662.

Grant, Lord, that such as I am, I may be conformed to Thy will; and that being in sickness I may glorify Thee in my sufferings. Without them I cannot arrive at glory; even Thou, O my Saviour, didst not will to reach thither without them. It was by the mark of Thy sufferings that Thou wert recognised by Thy disciples; and it is by their sufferings also that Thou recogniseth Thy disciples. Recognise me, then, for Thy disciple in the pains which I endure, both in my body and in my soul, for the sins which I have committed. And since nothing is well-pleasing to God, if it be not offered by Thee, unite my will to Thine, and my griefs to those Thou hast endured. Cause that mine become Thine. Unite me to Thyself; fill me with Thyself and Thy Holy Spirit. Enter into my soul and my heart, there to bear my sufferings, and to continue to endure in me what remains of Thy passion* which Thou art accomplishing in Thy members

* Col. i. 24.

until the perfect consummation of Thy body; so that, being full of Thee, it shall be no longer I that live and suffer, but Thou that livest and sufferest in me, O my Saviour! And thus having some small part in Thy sufferings, that Thou mayest fill me wholly with that glory which Thou hast acquired, and in which Thou livest with the Father and the Holy Spirit through all ages. So be it.

—Pensées, vol. i.

XXXIX.—A Litany. By Dr. John Donne, Dean of St. Paul's. 1631.

[This strangely obscure Litany, full of the quaint conceits and pedantry of the times, was written when Dr. Donne was in a consumption and nearing his end. It was used in worship at St. Paul's Cathedral.]

The Father

Father of Heaven, and Him by whom
It and us for it, and all else for us
Thou mad'st, and governest ever, come
And re-create me now grown ruinous.
   My heart is by dejection clay,
   And by self-murder red.
From this red earth, O Father, purge away
All vicious tincture, that new fashionëd
I may rise up from death, before I'm dead.

The Son.

O Son of God, who seeing two things,
Sin and Death, crept in which were never made,
By bearing *one* tryd'st with what stings
The other could Thine heritage invade;

O be Thou nailed unto my heart
And crucified again.
Part not from it, though it from Thee would part,
But let it be, by applying so Thy pain,
Drowned in Thy blood and in Thy passion slain.

THE HOLY GHOST.

O Holy Ghost, whose temple I
Am, but of mud walls and condensed dust,
And being sacrilegiously
Half wasted with youth's fires of pride and lust,
    Must with new storms be weather-beat,
    Double in my heart the flame,
Which let devout sad tears attend ; and let
(Though the glass lanthorn flesh do suffer maim),
Fire, sacrifice, priest, altar, be the same.

THE TRINITY.

O blessed, glorious Trinity,
Bones to philosophy but milk to faith,
Which as wise serpents diversely
Most slipperiness yet most entanglings hath,
As you distinguished, undistinct
By power, love, knowledge be,
Give me a such self-different instinct ;
Of these let all me elemented be,
Of power to love, to know, you unnumbered Three.

"It is difficult to realise what those emotional feelings were which could find wings and expression in these strains, or what the mind could be which found its recreations, during severe illness, in stringing together such perplexities of thought and language."—*Isabella L. Bird.*

XL.—**Another Prayer, by Dr. John Donne, Dean of St. Paul's.** Written shortly before his death, 31st March, 1631, and entitled

A Hymn to God the Father.

Wilt Thou forgive that sin, where I begun,
   Which was my sin, though it were done before ?
Wilt Thou forgive that sin, through which I run,
   And do run still, though still I do deplore ?
When Thou hast done, Thou hast not done,
                      For I have more.

Wilt Thou forgive that sin which I have won
   Others to sin, and made my sin their door ?
Wilt Thou forgive that sin, which I did shun
   A year or two, but wallowed in a score ?
When Thou hast done Thou hast not done,
                      For I have more.

I have a sin of fear, that when I've spun
   My last thread, I shall perish on the shore ;
But swear by Thyself, that at my death Thy Son
   Shall shine, as He shines now and heretofore,
And having done that, Thou hast done ;
                      I fear no more !

XLI.—**A Prayer in Sickness. By Dr. John Donne.**

O most mighty and merciful God, the God of all true sorrow and true joy too, of all fear and of all hope too, as Thou hast given me a repentance not to be repented of, so give me, O Lord, a fear of which I may not be afraid. Give me tender, and supple, and conformable affections, that as I joy with them that joy, and mourn with them that mourn, so may I fear with them that fear. In this sickness, in which there is danger, let me not, O Lord, go about to overcome the sense of that fear, so far as to pretermit the fitting and preparing of myself for the worst that may be feared—the passage out of this life. Many of Thy blessed martyrs have passed out of this life without any show of fear: but Thy most blessed Son Himself did not so. Thy martyrs were known to be but men, and therefore it pleased Thee to fill them with Thy spirit and Thy power, so that they did more than men: Thy Son was declared by Thee and by Himself to be God, and it was requisite that He should declare Himself to be Man also, in the weakness of man. Let me not, therefore, O my God, be ashamed of those fears, but let me feel them, to determine, where His fear did, in a present submitting to all Thy will. And when Thou shalt have inflamed and thawed my former coldnesses and indevotions with these heats, and quenched my former heats with these sweats of Thine, and rectified my former presumptions and negligences with these fears, be pleased, O Lord, as one made so by Thee, to think me fit for Thee; and whether it be Thy pleasure to dispose of this body, this garment, so as to put it to a further wearing in this world, or to lay it up in the common wardrobe, the grave, for the next, glorify Thyself in Thy choice now, and glorify it then with that glory which Thy Son our Saviour Jesus Christ hath purchased for them whom Thou makest partakers of His resurrection. Amen.

XLII.—*A Prayer of Francis Quarles, Author of "The Emblems," founded upon the text, Job xiii. 24, "Wherefore hidest Thou Thy face."* 1635.

    Why dost Thou shade Thy loving face? O why
    Does that eclipsing hand so long deny
    The sunshine of Thy soul-enlivening eye?

    Without that light, what light remains to me?
    Thou art my Life, my Way, my Light; in Thee
    I live, and move, and by Thy beams I see.

    Thou art my Life; if Thou dost turn away,
    My life's a thousand deaths; Thou art my Way;
    Without Thee, Lord, I travel not, but stray.

    My Light Thou art; without Thy glorious light
    Mine eyes are darkened with perpetual night;
    My God, Thou art my Way, my Life, my Light.

    Thou art my Way; I wander, if Thou fly:
    Thou art my Light; if hid, how blind am I!
    Thou art my Life; if Thou withdraw, I die.

    Mine eyes are blind and dark, I cannot see;
    To whom, or whither, should my darkness flee
    But to the Light? And who's that Light but Thee?

Francis Quarles. 1635.

My path is lost, my wandering steps do stray;
I cannot safely go, nor safely stay;
Whom should I seek but Thee, my Path, my Way?

O, I am dead; to whom shall I, poor I,
Repair? To whom shall my sad ashes fly
But Life? And where is Life but in Thine eye?

And yet Thou turn'st away Thy face, and fly'st me;
And yet I sue for grace and Thou deny'st me!
Speak, art Thou angry, Lord, or only try'st me?

Unscreen those heavenly lamps, or tell me why
Thou shad'st Thy face? Perhaps Thou think'st no eye
Can view those flames, and not drop down and die?

If that be all, shine forth, and draw Thee nigher;
Let me behold and die, for my desire
Is, phœnix-like, to perish in that fire.

Death-conquered Lazarus, was redeem'd by Thee,
If I am dead, Lord, set Death's pris'ner free.
Am I more spent, or moulder'd worse than he?

If my puff'd Life be out, give leave to tine*
My flameless snuff at that bright lamp of Thine;
O, what's Thy lamp the less for lighting mine?

If I have lost my path, great Shepherd, say,
Shall I still wander in a doubtful way?
Lord, shall a lamb of Israel's sheepfold stray?

Thou art the pilgrims' path, the blind man's eye,
The dead man's life; on Thee my hopes rely;
If Thou remove, I err, I grope, I die.

Disclose Thy sunbeams, close Thy wings and stay;
See, see how I am blind, and dead, and stray;
O Thou that art *my* Light, my Life, my Way.

* *I.e.* kindle, set on fire.

XLIII.—Another Prayer by Francis Quarles. 1635.

Great Shepherd of my soul, whose life was not too dear to rescue me, the meanest of Thy little flock, cast down Thy gracious eye upon the weakness of my nature, and behold it in the strength of Thy compassion; open mine eyes, that I may see that object which flesh cannot behold. Enlighten mine understanding, that I may clearly discern that truth which my ignorance cannot apprehend; rectify my judgment, that I may constantly resolve those doubts which my understanding cannot determine; and sanctify my will, that I may wisely choose that good which my deceived heart cannot desire; fortify my resolution, that I may constantly embrace that choice which my inconstancy cannot hold; weaken the strength of my corrupted nature, that I may struggle with my lusts and strive against the base rebellions of my flesh. Strengthen the weakness of my dejected spirit, that I may conquer myself, and still withstand the assaults of mine own corruption; moderate my delight in the things of this world, and keep my desires within the limits of Thy will. Let the points of my thoughts be directed to Thee, and let my hopes rest in the assurance of Thy favour: let not the fear of worldly loss dismay me, nor let the loss of the world's favour daunt me. Let my joy in Thee exceed all worldly grief, and let the love of Thee expel all carnal fear; let the multitudes of my offences be hid in the multitudes of Thy compassions, and let the reproachfulness of that death which Thy Son suffered for my sake, enable me to suffer all reproach for His sake. Let not my sin against Thy mercies remove Thy mercies from my sin; and let the necessity of my offences be swallowed up in the all-sufficiency of His merits; let not the foulness of my transgressions lead me to distrust, nor let the distrust of Thy pardon leave me in despair. Fix in my heart a filial love, that I may love Thee as a Father, and remove all servile fear from me, that Thou mayest behold me as a son. Be Thou my all-in-all, and let me fear nothing but to displease Thee; that, being freed from the fear of Thy wrath, I may live in the comfort of Thy promise, die in the fulness of Thy favour, and rise to the inheritance of an everlasting kingdom. Amen.

XLIV.—*An Evening Prayer. By Johann Lassenius.* 1636—1692.

[Johann Lassenius was pastor and professor at Copenhagen, and the author of various devotional works.]

O Lord God, our Father in Heaven, Lord of our life, Thy works are pure goodness and truth. Thou hast kept us in life this day and has shown us much loving kindness, and preserved us from evil: therefore our mouth is full of Thy praise. But we are ashamed before Thee, O God, for we have once more sinned against Thee this day: we have not trod unswervingly in Thy path of duty. Ah Lord! who can tell how oft he offendeth: forgive us even our secret faults. Help us to overcome them, O Thou Consolation of Israel, and dispel our misdeeds as a cloud, and our sins as the morning mist. Redeem us and purify our consciences from dead works through the cross of Thy Son Jesus Christ, and withdraw not Thy helping hand from us. Behold, O Blessed Lord, the night is gathering fast; the darkness surrounds us; leave us not, O Thou who art our Light: go not down upon our hearts, O Thou our Sun! Watch over and defend us, parents and children, our household and home, our health and wealth, and keep us from harm and danger. May we calmly rest on Thy unfathomable goodness, and may Thy Word be our lantern and our guiding star. Unto Thee we commend ourselves, for in Thee is our hope: continue to guard and succour our souls, and may we awake to-morrow, if it be Thy will, with joyful hearts ready to sing Thy praise. Hear us for Thy dear Son's sake. Amen.

XLV.—A Prayer of Thanksgiving. By Bishop Ken.
BORN 1637, DIED 1711.

Worthy art Thou, O Lord of heaven and earth, to receive glory and honour and power and might and majesty: for Thou hast created all things, and for Thy pleasure they are and were created. Thou hast made heaven, the heaven of heavens, with all the hosts of them; the earth, and all things therein, and the host of heaven praiseth Thee. Glory be to Thee, O Lord God Almighty, for creating man after Thine own image, and making so great a variety of creatures to minister to his use.

Glory be to Thee, O heavenly Father, for our being, and preservation, health and strength, understanding and memory, friends and benefactors, and for all our abilities of mind and body. Glory be to Thee for our competent livelihood, for the advantages of our education, for all known or unobserved deliverances, and for the guard which Thy holy angels keep over us, but, above all, glory be to Thee for giving Thy Son to die for our sins, and for all the spiritual blessings which He has purchased for us.

Glory be to Thee, O Lord, the only begotten Son, Jesus Christ, for Thine inexpressible love to lost mankind, in undertaking the wonderful work of our redemption and rescuing us from the slavery of sin and dominion of the devil: for descending, in order to accomplish this prodigy of goodness, from heaven, and putting on the form of a servant: for the heavenly doctrine which Thou didst preach for our instruction, the undoubted miracles which Thou didst work for our conviction, and Thy unblameable example to be our rule and pattern; for Thine agony and bloody sweat, the torments and anguish of Thy bitter passion; and Thy precious death and burial, ascension into heaven, and intercession for us at the right hand of the Father.

Glory be to Thee O Lord, O blessed Saviour, for all the miraculous gifts and graces which Thou didst bestow upon prophets, apostles, and evangelists, to fit them to convert the world: for inspiring them to write the holy scriptures and preach the Gospel among the nations, and for bringing the glad tidings to this land of our nativity—for those ordinary gifts, by which sincere Christians have in all ages been enabled to work out their salvation—for subduing our understanding, will, and affections to the obedience of faith and godliness—for infusing into our minds holy thoughts, and enkindling in our hearts pious desires—for all the spiritual strength and support, comfort and illumination which we receive from

Thee, and for all Thy preserving, restraining and sanctifying grace.

Blessing and honour, thanksgiving and praise be unto Thee O adorable Trinity, Father, Son, and Holy Ghost from all angels, all men, and all creatures for ever and ever. Amen.

XLVI.—A Prayer by Henry Vaughan (Silurist). 1650.

BEGGING.

King of Mercy, King of Love,
In whom I live, in whom I move,
Perfect what Thou hast begun,
Let no night put out this Sun;
Grant I may, my chief desire!
Long for Thee, to Thee aspire,
Let my youth, my bloom of dayes
Be my comfort, and Thy praise,
That hereafter, when I look
O'r the sullyed, sinful book,
I may find Thy hand therein
Wiping out my shame and sin.
O it is Thy only Art
To reduce a stubborn heart,
And since thine is victorie,
Strongholds should belong to Thee;
Lord then take it, leave it not
Unto my dispose or lot,
But since I would not have it mine,
O my God, let it be Thine!

From "Silex Scintillans." Fac-simile of First Edition, 1650, with Introduction by Rev. William Clare, B.A. Adelaide, 1885.

XLVII.—**A Private Prayer by Thomas Wilson, D.D., for fifty-eight years Bishop of Sodor and Man.** BORN 1633, DIED 1755.—*From* SACRA PRIVATA.

O God, almighty and merciful, let Thy fatherly kindness be upon all whom Thou hast made. Hear the prayer of all that call upon Thee; open the eyes of them that never pray for themselves; pity the sighs of such as are in misery; deal mercifully with them that are in darkness, and increase the number of the graces of such as fear and serve Thee daily. Preserve this land from the misfortunes of war; this Church from all dangerous errors; this people from forgetting Thee, their Lord and benefactor. Be gracious to all those countries that are made desolate by the sword, famine, pestilence, or persecution. Bless all persons and places to which Thy providence has made me a debtor: all who have been instrumental to my good by their assistance, advice, or example; and make me in my time useful to others.

Let none of those that desire my prayers want Thy mercy: but defend and comfort and conduct them through to their lives' end.

Glory be to God my Creator, glory be to Jesus my Redeemer, glory be to the Holy Ghost my Sanctifier, my Guide and Comforter; all love, all glory be to God Most High. Amen.

XLVIII.—Andrew Rykman's Prayer. 1674 (?)

Andrew Rykman's dead and gone;
  You can see his leaning slate
In the graveyard, and thereon
  Read his name and date.

"*Trust is truer than our fears,*"
  Runs the legend through the moss,
"*Gain is not in added years,*
  Nor in death is loss."

Still the feet that thither trod,
  All the friendly eyes are dim;
Only nature, now, and God
  Have a care for him.

There the dews of quiet fall,
  Singing birds and soft winds stray;
Shall the tender heart of all
  Be less kind than they?

What he was and what he is
  They who ask may haply find,
If they read this prayer of his
  Which he left behind.

Pardon, Lord, the lips that dare
Shape in words a mortal's prayer!
Prayer, that, when my day is done,
And I see its setting sun,
Shorn, and beamless, cold and dim,
Sink beneath the horizon's rim—
When this ball of rock and clay
Crumbles from my feet away,
And the solid shores of sense
Melt into the vague immense,

Father! I may come to Thee
Even with the beggar's plea,
As the poorest of Thy poor,
With my needs and nothing more.

Not as one who seeks his home
With a step assured I come;
Still behind the tread I hear
Of my life-companion, Fear,
Still a shadow deep and vast
From my westering feet is cast,
Wavering, doubtful, undefined,
Never shapen nor outlined;
From myself the fear has grown
And the shadow is my own.

Yet, O Lord, through all a sense
Of Thy tender providence
Stays my failing heart on Thee,
And confirms the feeble knee;
And, at times, my worn feet press
Spaces of cool quietness,
Lilied whiteness shone upon
Not by light of moon or sun.
Hours there be of inmost calm,
Broken but by grateful psalm,
When I love Thee more than fear Thee,
And Thy blessed Christ seems near me,
With forgiving look, as when
He beheld the Magdalen.
Well I know that all things move
To the spheral rhythm of love—
That to Thee, O Lord of all!
Nothing can of chance befall;

Child and seraph, mote and star,
Well Thou knowest what we are;
Through Thy vast creative plan,
Looking, from the worm to man,
There is pity in Thine eyes
But no hatred nor surprise.
Not in blind caprice of will,
Not in cunning sleight of skill,
Not for show of power, was wrought
Nature's marvel in Thy thought.
Never careless hand and vain
Smites these chords of joy and pain;
No immortal selfishness
Plays the game of curse and bless;
Heaven and earth are witnesses
That Thy glory goodness is.
Not for sport of mind and force
Hast Thou made Thy universe,
But as atmosphere and zone
Of Thy loving heart alone.
Man, who walketh in a show,
Sees before him, to and fro,
Shadow and illusion go:
All things flow and fluctuate
Now contract and now dilate.
In the welter of this sea,
Nothing stable is but Thee;
In this whirl of swooning trance
Thou alone art permanence;
All without Thee only seems,
All beside is choice of dreams.
Never yet in darkest mood
Doubted I that Thou wast good,
Nor mistook my will for fate,
Pain of sin for heavenly hate,—

Never dreamed the gates of pearl
Rise from out the burning marl,
Or that good can only live
Of the bad conservative;
And through counterpoise of hell
Heaven alone be possible.
For myself alone I doubt;
All is well, I know, without;
I alone the beauty mar,
I alone the music jar.
Yet, with hands by evil stained,
And an ear by discord pained,
I am groping for the keys
Of the heavenly harmonies;
Still within my heart I bear
Love for all things good and fair.
Hands of want or souls in pain
Have not sought my door in vain;
I have kept my fealty good
To the human brotherhood;
Scarcely have I asked in prayer
That which others might not share.
I, who hear with secret shame
Praise that paineth more than blame,
Rich alone in favours lent,
Virtuous by accident,
Doubtful where I fain would rest,
Frailest when I seem the best,
Only strong for lack of test,—
What am I, that I should press
Special pleas of selfishness,
Coolly mounting into heaven
On my neighbour unforgiven?
Ne'er to me, howe'er disguised,
Comes a saint unrecognised;

Never fails my heart to greet
Noble deed with warmer beat;
Halt and maimed, I own not less
All the grace of holiness;
Nor, through shame or self-distrust,
Less I love the pure and just.

Lord, forgive these words of mine;
What have I that is not Thine?
Whatsoe'er I fain would boast
Needs Thy pitying pardon most.
Thou, O Elder Brother! who
In Thy flesh our trial knew,
Thou, who hast been touched by these
Our most sad infirmities,
Thou alone the gulf canst span
In the dual heart of man,
And between the soul and sense
Reconcile all difference,
Change the dream of me and mine,
For the truth of Thee and Thine,
And, through chaos, doubt, and strife,
Interfuse Thy calm of life.
Haply, thus by Thee renewed,
In Thy borrowed goodness, good,
Some sweet morning yet in God's
Dim, æonian periods,
Joyful I shall wake to see
Those I love who rest in Thee,
And to them in Thee allied
Shall my soul be satisfied.

Scarcely Hope that shaped for me
What the future life may be.
Other lips may well be bold;

Like the publican of old,
I can only urge the plea,
"Lord, be merciful to me!"
Nothing of desert I claim;
Unto me belongeth shame.
Not for me the crowns of gold,
Palms, and harpings manifold;
Not for erring eye and feet,
Jasper wall and golden street.
What Thou wilt, O Father, give!
All is gain that I receive.
If my voice I may not raise
In the elders' song of praise,
If I may not, sin-defiled,
Claim my birthright as a child,
Suffer it that I to Thee
As an hired servant be;
Let the lowliest task be mine,
Grateful, so the work be Thine;
Let me find the humblest place
In the shadow of Thy grace;
Blest to me were any spot
Where temptation whispers not.
If there be some weaker one,
Give me strength to help him on;
If a blinder soul there be
Let me guide him nearer Thee.
Make my mortal dreams come true,
With the work I fain would do;
Clothe with life the weak intent,
Let me be the thing I meant;
Let me find in Thy employ
Peace that dearer is than joy;
Out of self to love be led,
And to heaven acclimated,

Until all things sweet and good
Seem my natural habitude.

So we read the prayer of him
  Who, with John of Labadie,*
Trod, of old, the oozy rim
  Of the Zuyder Zee.

Thus did Andrew Rykman pray.
  Are we wiser, better grown
That we may not, in our day,
  Make his prayer our own?
—J. G. WHITTIER.

* "There was a sect of the Labadists, who believed in the Divine Commission of John De Labadie, a Roman Catholic priest converted to Protestantism, enthusiastic, eloquent and evidently sincere, in his special calling and election to separate the true and living members of the Church of Christ from the formalism and hypocrisy of the ruling sects. . . Labadie died in 1674, at Altona, in Denmark, maintaining his testimonies to the last."

XLIX.—**A Prayer of William Law, the Author of "A Serious Call to a Devout and Holy Life."** Dr. Johnson said of this work, that it first led to his thinking in earnest of religion. 1686—1761.

O God, who madest me for Thyself, to show forth Thy goodness in me, manifest, I humbly beseech Thee, the life-giving power of Thy holy nature within me; help me to such a true and living faith

* Note to Whittier's poem, "The Pennsylvania Pilgrim."

in Thee, such strength of hunger and thirst after the birth, life, and spirit of Thy holy Jesus in my soul, that all that is within me may be turned from every inward thought or outward wish that is not Thee, Thy holy Jesus, and heavenly working in my soul. Amen.

L.—A Prayer by Dr. Philip Doddridge, for Divine Guidance in dispensing Gifts. 1702—1751.

I adore Thee, O Thou God of Grace, if, while I am thus speaking to Thee, I feel the love of Thy creatures arising in my soul, if I feel my heart opening to embrace my brethren of mankind! Oh, make me Thy faithful almoner in distributing to them all that Thou hast lodged in my hand for their relief! And in determining what is my own share, may I hold the balance with an equal hand, and judge impartially between myself and them! The proportion Thou allowest may I thankfully take to myself and those who are immediately mine! The rest may I distribute with wisdom, and fidelity and cheerfulness! Guide mine hand, O ever-merciful Father, while Thou dost me the honour to make me Thine instrument in dealing out a few of Thy bounties, that I may bestow them where they are most needed, and where they will answer the best end! And, if it be Thy gracious will, do Thou multiply the seed sown; prosper me in my worldly affairs, that I may have more to impart to them that need it, and thus lead me on to everlasting plenty and everlasting benevolence! There may I meet with many to whom I have been an affectionate benefactor on earth, and, if it be Thy blessed will, with many whom I have also been the means of conducting into the path of that blissful abode! There may they entertain me in their habitations of glory! And in Time and Eternity, do Thou, Lord, accept the praise of all, through Jesus Christ, at whose feet I would bow, and at whose feet, after the most useful course, I would at last die, with as much humility as if I were then exerting the first act of faith upon Him, and never had an opportunity, by one tribute of obedience and gratitude in the services of life, to approve its sincerity. Amen.

LI.—Prayer by Dr. Samuel Johnson, when "he purposed to apply vigorously to study, particularly of the Greek and Italian tongues." JULY 25, 1776.

O God who hast ordained that whatever is to be desired should be sought by labour, and who, by Thy blessing, bringest honest labour to good effect; look with mercy upon my studies and endeavours. Grant me, O Lord, to design only what is lawful and right; and afford me calmness of mind and steadiness of purpose, that I may so do Thy will in this short life as to obtain happiness in the world to come, for the sake of Jesus Christ our Redeemer. Amen.

LII.—Another Prayer, "against inquisitive and perplexing thoughts." August 12, 1784.

O Lord, my maker and protector, who hast graciously sent me into this world to work out my salvation, enable me to drive from me all such unquiet and perplexing thoughts as may mislead or hinder me in the practice of those duties which Thou hast required. When I behold the works of Thy hands and consider the course of Thy providence, give me grace always to remember that Thy thoughts are not my thoughts nor Thy ways my ways. And while it shall please Thee to continue me in this world, where much is to be done and little to be known, teach me by Thy Holy Spirit to withdraw my mind from unprofitable and dangerous inquiries, from difficulties vainly curious, and doubts impossible to be solved. Let me rejoice in the light which Thou hast imparted; let me serve Thee with active zeal and humble confidence, and wait with patient expectation for the time in which the soul which Thou receivest, shall be satisfied with knowledge. Grant this, O Lord, for Jesus Christ's sake. Amen.

LIII.—The following Prayer is stated by Dr. Strahan—a former Vicar of Islington, who published a collection of Prayers under the title "Prayers and Meditations of Dr. Samuel Johnson"—to have been composed and used by Dr. Johnson previous to his receiving the Sacrament of the Lord's Supper, on Sunday, December 5, 1784.

Almighty and most merciful Father, I am now as to human eyes it seems, about to communicate for the last time* the death of Thy Son Jesus Christ our Saviour and Redeemer. Grant, O Lord, that my whole hope and confidence may be in His merits and Thy mercy; enforce and accept my imperfect repentance; make this communication available to the confirmation of my faith, the establishment of my hope, and the enlargement of my charity, and make the death of Thy Son Jesus Christ effectual to my redemption. Have mercy upon me and pardon the multitude of my offences. Bless my friends; have mercy upon all men. Support me by Thy Holy Spirit in the days of weakness and at the hour of death, and receive

* Dr. Johnson died on the 13th December, 1784.

me, at my death, to everlasting happiness, for the sake of Jesus Christ. Amen.

LIV.—A Missionary Prayer. From the Litany of the Moravian Church—of whom were the Fathers and Founders of Christian Missions throughout the world. A Prayer used in the Morning Service of that Church every Sunday. 1722.

Thou Light and Desire of all nations,
Watch over Thy messengers both by land and sea;
Prosper the endeavours of all Thy servants to spread the Gospel among the heathen nations;
Accompany the word of their testimony concerning Thy atonement, with demonstration of Thy spirit and of power;
Bless our congregations gathered from among the heathen;
Keep them as the apple of Thine eye;
Have mercy on Thy ancient covenant-people, the Jews; deliver them from their blindness;
And bring all nations to the saving knowledge of Thee:

Let the seed of Israel praise the Lord;
Yea, let all the nations praise Him:

Give to Thy people open doors to preach the

Gospel; and set them to Thy praise on earth. Amen.

LV.—A Self-Dedication Prayer. By Gerhard Tersteegen. 1724.

[Tersteegen, who has been called "the greatest poet of the mystical school of the seventeenth and eighteenth centuries," was a ribbon-weaver at Mülheim on the Ruhr. At the age of twenty-seven he wrote, in his own blood, the following form of "dedication of himself to Jesus." The depth and wisdom of his piety attracted multitudes of people from his own and other countries, to his house, "The Pilgrim's Cottage," to receive spiritual aid and counsel. He was the author of several devotional works full of calm, trustful surrender to God, and intense aspiration after holiness. One, entitled "Crumbs from the Master's Table," has been translated into English, and is well known.]

"To my Jesus."

"I dedicate myself to Thee, Christ Jesus, my only Saviour and my Bridegroom, to be Thine entire and everlasting possession. From this evening I reject with all my heart whatever right and power Satan, without right, gave me over myself, as one whom Thou, my Bridegroom by blood and my God, hast purchased through Thy fight with death, through Thy wrestling and bloody sweat in the Garden of Gethsemane, to be Thy possession and bride; for whom Thou hast burst the gates of hell and revealed to me the living heart of Thy Father. From this evening may my heart and all my love be offered up to Thee eternally in mental thanksgiving! From this day till eternity may

Thy will and not mine be done! Command, rule, and govern me! I give Thee full power over me, and promise, with Thy help and grace, that this my blood shall flow out to the last drop, sooner than, with will and knowledge, inwardly or outwardly, I be unfaithful or disobedient to Thee. Lo! Thou hast me altogether, Thou Friend of Souls! in modest virgin love I cling to Thee! Take not away Thy Holy Spirit from me; may Thy Spirit not turn from me; may Thy death-fight strengthen me! Yea. Amen. May Thy Spirit seal what in simplicity hath written,

"Thine unworthy possession,
"GERH. TERSTEEGEN."

"On Green Thursday evening, 1724."

LVI.—A Prayer by Gerhard Tersteegen. 1731.

TO THE RISEN AND ASCENDED SAVIOUR.

O Jesu, our Lord and King, who art highly exalted, in what glory has Thy course ended, how have the heavenly hosts welcomed Thee when Thou didst enter Thy Kingdom as Conqueror over Sin, Death, and Hell, and didst sit down on the right hand of God!

Ah! we strangers here on earth desire to partake in the joy of the heavenly ones, to bow the knee and give glory to Thee with them. Hosanna to the Son of David! Hosanna in the highest! Rule, O Jesus; send forth the sceptre out of Zion and bring all hearts under Thy sway. Thou hast passed into heaven, but we are yet dwelling upon earth; Thou hast completed Thy course, but we are yet treading the narrow and thorny way. Help us, and let all our steps be sanctified for the sake of Thy sorrowful path; may all Thy deeds, Thy self-denial, Thy prayers, Thy sufferings, hallow ours. Hold us by Thy strengthening hand, that we may walk fearlessly forward on the way that leads to heaven; not fainting beneath its toils, not standing still as beginners, but going on, through Thy Spirit, to holiness, perfection, and the final bliss. And to this end teach us the practice of true, earnest prayer from the heart, of quiet retirement, of patient waiting for Thy Spirit from on high. Jesu Christ, Thou our Head art glorified, and we are Thy members. Thou hast said, "When I am lifted up I will draw all men unto Me." Draw us then out of all our wickedness, our selfishness, our absorption in the things of sense and sight, into Thine own heavenly life that we may live with Thee where now Thou art. Let all worldliness be banished out of us, that we may not lose ourselves in what is temporal but seek after that which is eternal; so shall we with full hearts and true love, cleave to Thee alone, and occupy ourselves with that which alone can comfort and sustain us in the hour of trial or of death.

O Prince of Life! teach us to stand more boldly on Thy side, to face the world and all our enemies more courageously and not to let ourselves be dismayed by any storm of temptation; may our eyes be steadfastly fixed on Thee in fearless faith: may we trust Thee with perfect confidence that Thou wilt keep us, save us, and bring us through by the power of Thy grace and the riches of Thy mercy. Come and set up Thy kingdom in our hearts; unto Thee we submit ourselves and our powers, heart and mind, senses and thought,—all must be subject to Thee, all Thy faithful people must learn to be guided by the tokens of Thy good pleasure and walk as ever in Thy sight.

And O Mighty King! bring under Thy sway all who as yet rebel against Thee. Send out apostles and teachers who shall make known to sinners the greatness of Thy majesty and the greatness of Thy love, that Thy kingdom may be spread abroad even unto the ends of the world. Ah! when O Lord, wilt Thou come in Thy power, that the hearts of all nations may be turned unto Thee?

Awaken us from all indolence and dreaminess;

teach us to walk before Thee with burning lamps, with cheerful hearts, day by day expecting our summons home, that when it comes we may be found ready. Give us abundantly the oil of Thy Spirit and Thy Love, that we may be kept alert in constant watchfulness and unwearied prayer. Draw us heavenwards that we may every day mount thither in faith till we do so perfectly on that day when Thou dost call us home.

Bless all Thy children throughout the earth; mould them to Thy heavenly image, so that their holy conduct may draw many to Thee, and make them willing subjects to Thy rule. Strengthen all, strengthen each one, to be faithful to Thee unto the end.

O Lord we lay our sighs upon Thy heart; bring them, O Priest, to the Holy of holies, bring our prayers unto Thy Father, obtain a gracious hearing, seal Thy Word to our hearts, and fulfil all our desires. Amen.

LVII.—The Universal Prayer. By Alexander Pope. 1734.

["Concerning this poem, it may be proper to observe that some passages in the preceding essay "—' The Essay on Man '—"having been unjustly suspected of a tendency towards fate and naturalism, the Author composed this prayer as the sum of all to show that his system was founded on free-will, and terminated in piety; that the First Cause was as well the Lord and Governor of the universe as the Creator of it, and that, by submission to His Will (the great principle enforced throughout the

Essay) was not meant the suffering ourselves to be hurried along with a blind determination, but a religious acquiescence and confidence full of hope and immortality. To give all this the greater weight and reality, the poet chose for his model the Lord's Prayer, which, of all others, best deserves the title prefixed to this paraphrase."—WARBURTON.]

DEO OPT. MAX.

Father of all! in every age,
    In every clime adored,
By saint, by savage, and by sage,
    Jehovah, Jove, or Lord!

Thou Great First Cause, least understood;
    Who all my sense confined
To know but this, that thou art good,
    And that myself am blind;

Yet gave me in this dark estate,
    To see the good from ill;
And binding nature fast in fate
    Left free the human will.

What conscience dictates to be done,
    Or warns me not to do,
This, teach me more than hell to shun,
    That, more than heaven pursue.

What blessings Thy free bounty gives,
    Let me not cast away;
For God is paid when man receives,
    To enjoy is to obey.

Yet not to earth's contracted span
    Thy goodness led me bound,
Or think Thee Lord alone of man,
    When thousand worlds are round.

Let not this weak, unknowing hand
  Presume Thy bolts to throw,
And deal damnation round the land,
  On each I judge Thy foe.

If I am right, Thy grace impart
  Still in the right to stay;
If I am wrong, oh, teach my heart
  To find that better way.

Save me alike from foolish pride,
  Or impious discontent,
At aught Thy wisdom has denied,
  Or aught Thy goodness lent.

Teach me to feel another's woe,
  To hide the fault I see:
That mercy I to others show,
  That mercy show to me.

Mean though I am, not wholly so,
  Since quickened by Thy breath;
Oh, lead me wheresoe'r I go
  Through this day's life or death.

This day, be bread and peace my lot;
  All else beneath the sun,
Thou knowest if best bestowed or not;
  And let Thy will be done.

To Thee, whose temple is all space,
  Whose altar earth, sea, skies,
One chorus let all being raise,
  All natures incense rise!

LVIII.—**A Covenant and Prayer, by John Burn of Glasgow.**
1738.

["It was a custom among pious Scotch people to write out 'a covenant' in accordance with the theological notion that the promises of God, as recorded in the Scriptures, are conditional on certain terms on the part of man. The first bond, or oath, drawn up by the Scottish Reformers, and signed in 1557, was a covenant; the 'Confession of Faith,' drawn up in 1581, was also a covenant, the subscription to which was renewed from time to time; when the General Assembly of the Church of Scotland contracted with the Commissioners of the English Parliament in 1643 for uniformity of doctrine, worship, and discipline throughout Scotland, England, and Ireland 'according to the Word of God, and the example of the best reformed churches,' the instrument was 'the Solemn League and Covenant.'

"The idea of a covenant, as distinct from a contract (the former having no civil penalty necessarily following the infraction of it), being ingrained in the Scottish mind, it is not surprising that when a man found himself in an attitude 'to accept salvation on God's own terms,' as the phrase went, he should, taking the written Word of God as the first part of the covenant, enter into a written engagement to fulfil the second part, namely, his own moral and religious obligations. And as subscription to the 'Confession of Faith' was renewed from time to time, so with these 'covenants with God'—or 'dedications' as they were in later times called—it was customary to keep them in constant remembrance, and, at recurring intervals, or at great crises in the history of those who made them, to officially 'recognise' the covenant. It may interest those who are not familiar with this quaint old notion in religion to read a part of the covenant of John Burn."—"*Life of Sir George Burns, Bart.*"]

Luss, *June 25, 1738, Sabbath afternoon.*

O Lord God Almighty, I would in Thy presence humbly confess that iniquities greatly prevail against me, the power of conquering which, O Lord, Thou knowest is far beyond my feeble strength; but in Thee alone is my sufficiency. O perfect Thy strength in my weakness and deliver me from the love, the power, the stain and the guilt of all sin, original and actual. Alas! with what aggravated transgressions do I stand chargeable? ... I have, times and ways, O Lord, without number, broken all Thy Commandments, for which I deserve Thy wrath and fury to be poured out upon my soul and body to all eternity! But now, O most merciful God, I desire this afternoon to renounce the love and practice of every wicked way, and in Thy name and strength to devote myself soul and body to Thee, that I may be Thine in prosperity or adversity, in health or sickness, in time and through eternity. I desire to believe in God the Father, who sent the Son into the world on the gracious errand of man's salvation, as my God and Father, and in Jesus Christ as my only Lord and Redeemer whom I desire to embrace as the Lord my righteousness; and in the Holy Ghost as my sanctifier, and the applier of all Christ's purchase to my defiled and polluted soul, and whose quickening influences and Divine illumination I beseech Thee, Holy Father, to shed abroad into my soul, through the infinite merits of Jesus Christ, Thine only and well-beloved Son, in whom Thou art ever well pleased. ... O keep me by Thy mighty power through faith in Jesus Christ unto eternal life: for without Thee, this, like all my former resolutions and engagements, will become as the morning cloud and early dew, which soon passeth away. O Lord, renouncing all my own righteousness, all I have done or ever can do, I desire to embrace Thee in all Thy mediatory character, and henceforth desire to walk in Thy strength, making mention of Thy righteousness, even Thine only.

JOHN BURN.

Recognised at Stirling, May 12, 1750.
Recognised at Glasgow, April 8, 1780.

LIX.—A Prayer of Charles Wesley. 1740.

Jesu, lover of my soul,
  Let me to Thy bosom fly,
While the nearer waters roll,
  While the tempest still is high!
Hide me, O my Saviour, hide
  Till the storm of life is past,
Safe into the haven guide;
  O receive my soul at last!

Other refuge have I none;
  Hangs my helpless soul on Thee;
Leave, ah! leave me not alone,
  Still support and comfort me!
All my trust on Thee is stay'd,
  All my help from Thee I bring;
Cover my defenceless head
  With the shadow of Thy wing!

Wilt Thou not regard my call?
  Wilt Thou not accept my prayer?
Lo! I sink, I faint, I fall!
  Lo! on Thee I cast my care!

Reach me out Thy gracious hand!
  While I of Thy strength receive,
Hoping against hope I stand,
  Dying and behold I live.

Thou, O Christ, art all I want;
  More than all in Thee I find;
Raise the fallen, cheer the faint,
  Heal the sick and lead the blind!
Just and holy is Thy Name;
  I am all unrighteousness;
False and full of sin I am,
  Thou art full of truth and grace.

Plenteous grace with Thee is found,
  Grace to cover all my sin;
Let the healing streams abound;
  Make and keep me sure within!
Thou of Life the Fountain art,
  Freely let me take of Thee;
Spring Thou up within my heart!
  Rise to all Eternity!

LX.—A Prayer by Susanna Wesley, "the Mother of the Wesleys."

If to esteem and have the highest reverence for Thee, if constantly and sincerely to acknowledge Thee, the supreme, the only desirable God, be to love Thee,—I DO LOVE THEE! If to rejoice in Thy essential majesty and glory; if to feel a vital joy overspread and cheer the heart at each perception of Thy blessedness, at every thought that Thou art

God, and that all things are in Thy power; that there is none superior or equal to Thee; be to love Thee,—I DO LOVE THEE. If comparatively to despise and undervalue all the world contains, which is esteemed great, fair, or good; if earnestly and constantly to desire Thee, Thy favour, Thy acceptance, Thyself, rather than any or all things Thou hast created, be to love Thee,—I DO LOVE THEE.

[Susanna Wesley has more claim to be linked with Methodism than giving it its founders—namely, the claim of "that clear sense, vigorous intellect, supremacy of duty and firm conscientiousness, that meditative piety and holy living" that made her a noble woman, that helped to make John Wesley a noble man—the man he was—and Charles Wesley, one of the greatest poets of the Church.]

LXI.—A Prayer of Thomas Chatterton. 1752—1770.

THE RESIGNATION.

O God, whose thunder shakes the sky,
    Whose eye this atom globe surveys,
To Thee, my only rock, I fly,
    Thy mercy in Thy justice praise.

The mystic mazes of Thy will,
    The shadows of celestial light,
Are past the pow'r of human skill—
    But what th' Eternal acts, is right.

O teach me in this trying hour,
    When anguish swells the dewy tear,
To still my sorrows, own Thy pow'r,
    Thy goodness love, Thy justice fear.

If in this bosom ought but Thee,
  Encroaching sought a boundless sway,
Omniscience could the danger see,
  And Mercy took the cause away.

Then why, my soul, dost thou complain?
  Why, drooping, seek the dark recess?
Shake off the melancholy chain,
  For God created all to bless.

But ah! my breast is human still;
  The rising sigh, the falling tear,
My languid vitals' feeble rill
  The sickness of my soul declare.

But yet, with fortitude resign'd,
  I'll thank th' inflicter of the blow;
Forbid the sigh, compose my mind,
  Nor let the gush of mis'ry flow.

The gloomy mantle of the night,
  Which on my sinking spirit steals,
Will vanish at the morning light,
  Which God, my East, my Sun reveals.

LXII.—A Prayer of Robert Southey. 1774—1843.

Lord, who art merciful as well as just,
Incline Thine ear to me, a child of dust,
Not what I would, O Lord, I offer Thee,
    Alas! but what I can.
Father Almighty! who hast made me man,
And bade me look to Heaven, for Thou art there,
Accept my sacrifice and humble prayer.

> Four things which are not in Thy treasury,
> I lay before Thee, Lord, with this petition:
> My nothingness, my wants,
> My sins, and my contrition.

LXIII.—A Prayer by Bishop Richard Mant. 1776—1848.

> Son of God, to Thee I cry;
> By the holy mystery
> Of Thy dwelling here on earth,
> By Thy pure and holy birth,
> Lord, Thy presence let me see,
> Manifest Thyself to me.
>
> Lamb of God, to Thee I cry;
> By Thy bitter agony,
> By Thy pangs to us unknown,
> By Thy Spirit's parting groan,
> Lord, Thy presence let me see,
> Manifest Thyself to me.
>
> Prince of Life, to Thee I cry;
> By Thy glorious majesty,
> By Thy triumph o'er the grave,
> Meek to suffer, strong to save,
> Lord, Thy presence let me see,
> Manifest Thyself to me.
>
> Lord of Glory, God most high,
> Man exalted to the sky,
> With Thy love my bosom fill;
> Prompt me to perform Thy will;
> Then Thy glory I shall see,
> Thou wilt bring me home to Thee.

LXIV.—**A Prayer of Thomas Moore.** 1779—1852.

THE WIPER AWAY OF TEARS.
"He healeth the broken in heart."—PSALM cxlvii. 3.

O Thou! who dry'st the mourner's tear,
   How dark this world would be,
If, when deceiv'd and wounded here,
   We could not fly to Thee!
The friends, who in our sunshine live,
   When winter comes are flown;
And he, who has but tears to give
   Must weep those tears alone.
But Thou wilt heal that broken heart,
   Which, like the plants that throw
Their fragrance from the wounded part,
   Breathes sweetness out of woe.

When joy no longer soothes nor cheers,
   And e'en the hope that threw
A moment's sparkle o'er our tears
   Is dimm'd and vanish'd too;
Oh! who would bear life's stormy doom,
   Did not Thy wing of love
Come, brightly wafting through the gloom,
   Our Peace-branch from above?
Then sorrow, touch'd by Thee, grows bright,
   With more than rapture's ray,
As darkness shows us worlds of light
   We never saw by day!

LXV.—**A Litany. By Sir Robert Grant.** 1785—1838.

Saviour, when in dust to Thee
Low we bend the adoring knee;
When, repentant, to the skies
Scarce we lift our weeping eyes;

Oh, by all the pains and woe
Suffered once for man below,
Bending from Thy throne on high,
Hear our solemn Litany!

By Thy helpless infant years,
By Thy life of want and tears;
By Thy days of sore distress
In the savage wilderness;
By the dread mysterious hour
Of the insulting tempter's power;
Turn, oh, turn a favouring eye,
Hear our solemn Litany!

By the sacred grief that wept
O'er the grave where Lazarus slept;
By the boding tears that flowed
Over Salem's loved abode;
By the anguished sigh that told
Treachery lurked within Thy fold;
From Thy seat above the sky
Hear our solemn Litany!

By Thine hour of dire despair;
By Thine agony of prayer;
By the cross, the nail, the thorn,
Piercing spear, and torturing scorn;
By the gloom that veiled the skies
O'er the dreadful sacrifice;
Listen to our humble cry,
Hear our solemn Litany.

By Thy deep expiring groan;
By the sad sepulchral stone;
By the vault, whose dark abode,
Held in vain the rising God;

> Oh! from earth to heaven restored,
> Mighty re-ascended Lord,
> Listen, listen to the cry
> Of our solemn Litany.

LXVI.—Dr. Thomas Arnold's Prayer, for his own daily use before entering upon his school duties at Rugby. 1795—1842.

O Lord, I have a busy world around me; eye, ear, and thought will be needed for all my work to be done in that busy world. Now, ere I enter upon it, I would commit eye, ear, and thought to Thee! Do Thou bless them and keep their work Thine, such as, through Thy natural laws, my heart beats and my blood flows without any thought of mine for them, so my spiritual life may hold on its course at those times when my mind cannot consciously turn to Thee to commit each particular thought to Thy service. Hear my prayer for my dear Redeemer's sake. Amen.

LXVII.—Prayer read every morning by Dr. Arnold in the sixth form at Rugby.

O Lord, who, by Thy holy apostle, hast taught us to do all things in the name of the Lord Jesus and to Thy glory, give Thy blessing, we pray Thee, to this our daily work, that we may do it in faith, and heartily, as to the Lord, and not unto men. All our powers of body and mind are Thine, and we would fain devote them to Thy service. Sanctify them and the work in which they are engaged; let us not be slothful, but fervent in spirit, and do Thou, O Lord, so bless our efforts, that they may bring forth in us the fruits of true wisdom. Strengthen the faculties of our minds and dispose us to exert them, but let us always remember to exert them for Thy glory, and for the furtherance of Thy kingdom, and save us from all pride, and vanity, and reliance upon our own power or wisdom. Teach us to seek after truth, and enable us to gain it; but grant that we may ever speak the truth in love—that, while we know earthly things, we may know Thee, and be known by Thee, through and in Thy Son Jesus Christ. Give us this day Thy Holy Spirit, that we may be Thine in body and spirit in all our work and all our refreshments, through Jesus Christ, Thy Son, our Lord. Amen.

LXVIII.—Whittier's Prayer. 1807—1892.

Dear Lord and Father of mankind,
   Forgive our feverish ways!
Reclothe us in our rightful mind;
In purer lives Thy service find,
   In deeper reverence, praise.

In simple trust, like theirs who heard,
    Beside the Syrian sea,
The gracious calling of the Lord ;
Let us, like them, without a word,
    Rise up and follow Thee.

O, Sabbath rest by Galilee !
    O calm of hills above,
Where Jesus knelt to share with Thee
The silence of Eternity
    Interpreted by love !

With that deep hush subduing all
    Our words and works that drown
The tender whisper of Thy call,
As noiseless let Thy blessing fall
    As fell Thy manna down.

Drop Thy still dews of quietness
    Till all our strivings cease ;
Take from our souls the strain and stress ;
And let our ordered lives confess
    The beauty of Thy peace.

Breathe through the pulses of desire
    Thy coolness and Thy balm ;
Let sense be dumb, its heats expire ;
Speak through the earthquake, wind, and fire,
    O still small voice of calm !

LXIX.—The Cry of the Human. By Elizabeth Barrett Browning. 1809—1861.

I.

"There is no God," the foolish saith,
    But none, "There is no sorrow,"
And nature oft the cry of faith,
    In bitter need, will borrow ;

Eyes, which the preacher could not school,
  By wayside graves are raisëd,
And lips say, "God be pitiful,"
  Who ne'er said, "God be praisëd."
                    Be pitiful, O God!

II.

The tempest stretches from the steep
  The shadow of its coming,
The beasts grow tame and near us creep,
  As help were in the human;
Yet, while the cloud-wheels roll and grind,
  We spirits tremble under—
The hills have echoes, but we find
  No answer for the thunder.
                    Be pitiful, O God!

III.

The battle hurtles on the plains,
  Earth feels new scythes upon her:
We reap our brothers for the wains,
  And call the harvest—honour:
Draw face to face, front line to line,
  One image all inherit,—
Then kill, curse on, by that same sign,
  Clay—clay, and spirit—spirit.
                    Be pitiful, O God!

IV.

The plague runs festering through the town,
  And never a bell is tolling,
And corpses, jostled 'neath the moon,
  Nod to the dead-cart's rolling;
The young child calleth for the cup,
  The strong man brings it weeping;
The mother from her babe looks up
  And shrieks away its sleeping!
                    Be pitiful, O God!

V.

The plague of gold strikes far and near,
    And deep and strong it enters;
This purple chimar which we wear,
    Makes madder than the centaur's;
Our thoughts grow blank, our words grow strange,
    We cheer the pale gold-diggers,
Each soul is worth so much on 'Change,
    And marked, like sheep, with figures.
                  Be pitiful, O God!

VI.

The curse of gold upon the land
    The lack of bread enforces;
The rail-cars snort from strand to strand,
    Like none of Death's white horses;
The rich preach "rights" and "future days,"
    And hear no angel scoffing,
The poor die mute, with starving gaze
    On corn-ships in the offing.
                  Be pitiful, O God!

VII.

We meet together at the feast,
    To private mirth betake us;
We stare down in the winecup, lest
    Some vacant chair should shake us;
We name delight, and pledge it round—
    "It shall be ours to-morrow!"
God's seraphs, do your voices sound
    As sad, in naming sorrow?
                  Be pitiful, O God!

VIII.

We sit together, with the skies,
    The steadfast skies, above us,
We look into each other's eyes,
    "And how long will you love us?"

The eyes grow dim with prophecy,
   The voices, low and breathless,—
"Till death us part!"—O words, to be
   Our *best*, for love the deathless.
                      Be pitiful, O God!

IX.

We tremble by the harmless bed
   Of one loved and departed;
Our tears drop on the lips that said
   Last night "Be stronger-hearted!"
O God,—to clasp those fingers close,
   And yet to feel so lonely!
To see a light upon such brows,
   Which is the day-light only!
                      Be pitiful, O God!

X.

The happy children come to us,
   And look up in our faces;
They ask us: "Was it thus, and thus,
   When we were in their places?"
We cannot speak; we see anew
   The hills we used to live in,
And feel our mother's smile pass through
   The kisses she is giving.
                      Be pitiful, O God!

XI.

We pray together at the kirk
   For mercy, mercy solely;
Hands weary with the evil work,
   We lift them to the Holy.
The corpse is calm below our knee,
   Its spirit, bright before Thee—
Between them, worse than either, we—
   Without the rest or glory.
                      Be pitiful, O God!

XII.

We leave the communing of men,
  The murmur of the passions,
And live alone, to live again,
  With endless generations;
Are we so brave?—The sea and sky
  In silence lift their mirrors,
And, glassed therein, our spirits high
  Recoil from their own terrors.
          Be pitiful, O God!

XIII.

We sit on hills our childhood wist,
  Woods, hamlets, streams beholding:
The sun strikes through the farthest mist,
  The city's spire to golden;
The city's golden spire it was,
  When hope and health were strongest,
But now it is the churchyard grass
  We look upon the longest.
          Be pitiful, O God!

XIV.

And soon all vision waketh dull;
  Men whisper, "He is dying;"
We cry no more "Be pitiful!"
  We have no strength for crying;
No strength, no need. Then, soul of mine,
  Look up and triumph rather—
Lo, in the depth of God's Divine,
  The Son adjures the Father.
          BE PITIFUL, O GOD!

LXX.—**Prayer of Dr. Thomas Chalmers. On Friendship.**
1816.

[In a letter to his intimate friend, Mr. Thomas Smith (January, 1816) Dr. Chalmers wrote: " I shall not take up the remainder of my time wit, any topic of observation whatever, but recollecting that Dr. Samuel

Johnson often wrote his prayers, and found this a more powerfully devotional exercise than if he had said them, I entreat my dear friend's indulgence if I do the same at present; and as a blessing on that tender intimacy to which God, who turneth the heart of man whithersoever He will, has turned our hearts, is the great burden of my present aspiration to Heaven, I send it to you that you may, if you approve, join in it, and that the promise may be realised in us, that if two shall agree, touching anything they shall ask it shall be done unto them."—" Dr. Hanna's Memoirs of Thomas Chalmers, D.D., LL.D."]

O God, do Thou look propitiously on our friendship. Do Thou purify it from all that is base, and sordid, and earthly. May it be altogether subordinated to the love of Thee. May it be the instrument of great good to each of our souls. May it sweeten the path of our worldly pilgrimage; and after death has divided us for a season, may it find its final blessedness and consummation at the right hand of Thine everlasting throne.

We place ourselves before Thee as the children of error. O grant that in Thy light we may clearly see light; for this purpose let our eye be single. Let our intention to please Thee in all things be honest. With the childlike purpose of being altogether what Thou wouldst have us to be, may we place ourselves before Thy Bible, that we may draw our every lesson, and our every comfort out of it. O that Thy spirit may preside over our daily reading of Thy word, and that the word of our blessed Saviour may dwell in us richly in all wisdom.

O save us from the deceitfulness of this world. Forbid that any one of its pleasures should sway us aside from the path of entire devotedness to Thee. Give us to be vigilant, and cautious, and fearful. May we think of Thine eye as at all times upon us; and may the thought make us to tremble at the slightest departure from that narrow way of sanctification which leads to the house of our Father who is in Heaven.

We desire to honour the Son even as we honour the Father. We act in the presumption of our hearts when we think of placing ourselves before Thee in our own righteousness. Draw us to Christ. Make Him all our desire and all our salvation. Give remission of sins out of His blood. Give strength out of His fulness; and, crowned with all might, may we not only be fellow-helpers to each other, but may the work of turning sons and daughters unto righteousness, prosper in our hands. All we ask is for the sake of Thy Son and our Saviour, Jesus Christ. Amen.

LXXI.—**Another Prayer by Dr. Chalmers. On the National Fast Day, 22nd February, 1832, appointed for Prayer against the approach of Cholera.**

Do Thou, O Lord, ward off from us the further inroads of that desolating plague, which, in its mysterious progress over the face of the earth, has made such fearful ravages among the families of other lands. Hitherto, O God, hast Thou dealt mildly and mercifully with the city of our own habitation. Do Thou pour out the spirit of grace and supplication upon its inhabitants, and spare them, if it be Thy blessed will, the inflictions of that wrath which is so rightfully due to a careless and ungodly generation.

We pray, O Lord, in a more especial manner, for those patriotic men whose duty calls them to a personal encounter with this calamity, and who, braving all the hazards of infection, may be said to stand between the living and the dead. Save them from the attacks of disease; save them from the obloquies of misconception and prejudice; and may they have the blessings and acknowledgments of a grateful community to encourage them in their labours.

Above all, we pray, O God, that the infidelity which places all its reliance on secondary causes, may never sway either the councils of this city or the councils of this nation.* May there at all times be the public recognition of a God in the midst of us. And let not the defiance or levity of irreligious men ever

---

* In the House of Commons the recognition of God's hand in the pestilence had been denounced by one member as "cant, hypocrisy, and humbug."

tempt us to forget that mighty, unseen Being, who has all the forces of nature at His command—who sits behind the elements that He has formed, and gives birth and movement and continuance to all things.

<small>Quoted in Hanna's "Memoirs of Chalmers," vol. ii., p. 249.</small>

LXXII.—**The Story of a Prayer for Lord Byron.** 1821.

John Sheppard, of Frome, in Somerset, the friend of John Foster, and the author of "Thoughts at Seventy-nine," "Thoughts on Private Devotion," &c., wrote to Lord Byron thus:—

"Frome, Somerset, November 21st, 1821.

"To the Right Hon. Lord Byron, Pisa.

"MY LORD,—More than two years since, a lovely and beloved wife was taken from me by a lingering disease, after a very short union. She possessed unvarying gentleness and fortitude, and a piety so retiring as rarely to disclose itself in words; but so influential as to produce uniform benevolence of conduct. In the last hour of life, after a farewell look on a lately born and only infant, for whom she had evinced inexpressible affection, her last whispers were, "God's happiness! God's happiness!' Since the second anniversary of her decease, I have read some papers which no one had seen during her life, and which contained her most secret thoughts. I am induced to communicate to your lordship a passage from these papers, which, there is no doubt, refers to yourself, as I have more than once heard the writer mention your agility on the rocks at Hastings.

"' O, my God, I take encouragement from the assurance of Thy word, to pray to Thee in behalf of one for whom I have been lately much interested. May the person to whom I allude (and who is now, we fear, as much distinguished for his neglect of Thee, as for the transcendent talents Thou hast bestowed on him) be awakened to a sense of his own danger, and led to seek that peace of mind, in a proper sense of religion, which he has found this world's enjoyments unable to procure. Do Thou grant that his future example may be productive of far more extensive benefit, than his past conduct and writings have been of evil. And may the Sun of Righteousness, which we trust will, at some future period, arise upon him, be bright in proportion to the darkness of those clouds which guilt has raised, and soothing in proportion to the keenness of that agony which the punishment of his vices has inflicted on him. May the hope that the sincerity of my own efforts for the attainment of holiness, and the approval of my own love to the great Author of religion, render this prayer, and every other for the welfare of mankind, more efficacious, and cheer me in the path of duty. But let me not forget that, while we are permitted to animate ourselves to exertion by every innocent motive, these are but the lesser streams which may serve to increase the current, but which, deprived of the great Fountain of Good (a deep conviction of inborn sin, and firm belief in the efficacy of Christ's death for the salvation of those who trust in Him, and really seek to serve him), would soon dry up and leave us as barren of every virtue as before.

"' Hastings, July 31st, 1814.'

"There is nothing, my lord, in this extract, which, in a literary sense, can at all interest you. But it may, perhaps, appear to you worthy of reflection, how deep and expansive a concern for the happiness of others, a Christian faith can awaken in the midst of youth and prosperity. Here is nothing poetical and splendid, as in the expostulatory homage of M. de Lamartine; but here is the 'sublime,' my lord, for this intercession was offered on your account to the Supreme Source of happiness. It sprang from a faith more confirmed than that of the French poet; and from a charity which, in combination with faith, showed itself unimpaired amidst the languor and pains of approaching dissolution. I will hope that a prayer which, I am sure, was deeply sincere, may not be always unavailing.

"It would add nothing, my lord, to the fame with which your genius has surrounded you, for an unknown and obscure individual to express his admiration of it. I would rather be numbered with those who wish and pray that wisdom from above, and peace, and joy, may enter such a mind."

To this communication, Lord Byron sent the following reply:—

"Pisa, December 8th, 1821.

"Sir,—I have received your letter. I need not say that the extract which it contains has affected me, because it would imply a want of all feeling to have read it with indifference. Though I am not quite sure that it was intended by the writer for me, yet the date, the place where it was written, with some other circumstances which you mention, render the allusion probable. But, for whomsoever it was meant, I have read it with all the pleasure which can arise from so melancholy a topic. I say pleasure, because your brief and simple picture of the life and demeanour of this excellent person, whom I trust that you will again meet, cannot be contemplated without the admiration due to her virtues, and her pure and unpretending piety. Her last moments were particularly striking; and I do not know that, in the course of reading the story of mankind, and still less in my observations upon the existing portion, I ever met with anything so unostentatiously beautiful. Indisputably, the firm believers in the gospel have a great advantage over all others: for this simple reason—that, if true, they have their reward hereafter; and if there be no hereafter, they can be but with the infidel in his eternal sleep, having had the assistance of an exalted hope through life, without subsequent disappointment, since (at the worst of them) out of nothing nothing can arise; not even sorrow. . . .

"But my business is to acknowledge your letter and not to make a dissertation. I am obliged to you for your good wishes; and more obliged by the extract from the papers of the beloved object whose qualities you so well described in a few words. I can assure you that all the fame which ever cheated humanity into higher notions of its own importance, would never weigh on my mind against the pure and pious interest which a virtuous being may be pleased to take in my welfare. In this point of view, I would not exchange the prayer of the deceased in my behalf, for the united glory of Homer, Cæsar, and Napoleon, could they be accumulated upon a living head. Do me the justice to suppose that 'video meliora proboque' however the 'deteriora sequor'* may have been applied to my conduct. I have the honour to be, your obedient servant,

"BYRON."

Contributed by Rev. WM. DORLING *to* "Sunday Magazine," 1879.

LXXIII.—**A Prayer by Matthew Arnold.** 1822—1888.

STAGIRIUS.

[Stagirius was a young monk to whom St. Chrysostom addressed three books, and of whom those books give an account. They will be found in the first volume of the Benedictine Edition of St. Chrysostom's Works.]

---

* "Video meliora proboque deteriora sequor" = "I see and approve the better things, I follow the worse."—ED.]

Thou, who dost dwell alone—
Thou, who dost know thine own—
Thou, to whom all are known
From the cradle to the grave—
    Save, oh ! save
From the world's temptations,
    From tribulations,
From that fierce anguish
Wherein we languish,
From that torpor deep
Wherein we lie asleep
Heavy as death, cold as the grave,
    Save, oh ! save.

When the soul growing clearer
  Sees God no nearer ;
When the soul, mounting higher,
  To God comes no nigher,
But the arch-fiend Pride
Mounts at her side,
Foiling her high emprise,
Sealing her eagle eyes,
And, when she fain would soar,
Makes idols to adore,
Changing the pure emotion
Of her high devotion,
To a skin-deep sense
Of her own eloquence ;
Strong to deceive, strong to enslave—
    Save, oh ! save.

From the ingrain'd fashion
Of this earthly nature
That mars thy creature :

From grief that is but passion,
From mirth that is but feigning,
From tears that bring no healing,
From wild and weak complaining
  Thine old strength revealing,
    Save, oh! save.
From doubt, where all is double,
Where wise men are not strong;
Where comfort turns to trouble,
Where just men suffer wrong;
Where sorrow treads on joy,
Where sweet things soonest cloy;
Where faiths are built on dust,
Where love is half mistrust,
Hungry, and barren, and sharp as the sea—
    Oh! set us free.
O let the false dream fly
Where our sick souls do lie,
  Tossing continually!
    O where Thy voice doth come
    Let all doubts be dumb,
    Let all words be mild,
    All strifes be reconciled.
    All pains beguiled!
    Light bring no blindness,
    Love no unkindness,
    Knowledge no ruin,
    Fear no undoing,
    From the cradle to the grave,
      Save, oh! save.

From "Early Poems." By Matthew Arnold. Macmillan & Co. 1895.

LXXIV.—**A Hymn of Prayer. By Sir John Bowring.**
1825.

 From the recesses of a lowly spirit
 Our humble prayer ascends; O Father, hear it!
 Upsoaring on the wings of awe and meekness,
      Forgive its weakness!

 I know, I feel, how mean and how unworthy
 The trembling sacrifice I pour before Thee;
 What can I offer in Thy presence holy,
      But sin and folly?

 For in Thy sight—who every bosom viewest—
 Cold are our warmest vows, and vain our truest:
 Thoughts of a hurrying hour; our lips repeat them,
      Our hearts forget them.

 We see Thy hand—it leads us, it supports us;
 We hear Thy voice—it counsels and it courts us;
 And then we turn away; and still Thy kindness
      Forgives our blindness.

 And still Thy rain descends, Thy sun is glowing,
 Fruits ripen round, flowers are beneath us blowing,
 And, as if man were some deserving creature,
      Joys cover nature.

 Oh, how long-suffering, Lord! but Thou delightest
 To win with love the wandering; Thou invitest,
 By smiles of mercy, not by frowns or terrors,
      Man from his errors.

 Who can resist Thy gentle call, appealing
 To every generous thought and grateful feeling?
 That voice paternal—whispering, watching ever,
      My bosom?—never.

Father and Saviour! plant within each bosom
The seeds of holiness, and bid them blossom
In fragrance and in beauty bright and vernal,
                And spring eternal.

Then place them in those everlasting gardens,
Where angels walk and seraphs are the wardens,
Where every flower that creeps through death's
    dark portal
                Becomes immortal.

LXXV.—"A Cry from the Depths." By Adolphe Monod. 1826.

[In 1826, Adolphe Monod became the first pastor of a French colony in Naples, and "it was when he was called for the first time to fulfil the serious duty of instructing men in religious truth, that he was startled to discover how inadequate were his own convictions. He then passed through the great crisis of his spiritual life. . . . He found God after an agonizing spiritual conflict . . . passing like Pascal, through one of those soul vigils, one of those wrestlings all the night, which leave the combatant, to use Monod's own words, *vainqueur, mais tout meurtri ; tout meurtri, mais vainqueur.*

"Can we not catch an echo of the bitterness of soul through which he himself had passed in this concluding passage from his first sermon?"— E. de Pressensé, D.D., "Contemporary Portraits," p. 163.]

O God! who humblest only that Thou mayest lift up, who troublest only to calm, who dost shake only to stablish and settle, we bow to the sentence which condemns us. We accept it with penitence and tears. Hide nothing from us of our misery. Shed abroad in our souls Thy pure and searching light, that we may see ourselves as we truly are! And at such a sight let there rise at once from this whole congregation, a cry of surprise and anguish which shall rend the atmosphere of indifference around us, which shall reach Thy ear and move Thy fatherly compassion towards us, so that, renouncing henceforward all our self-esteem, humbled with a deep humility, believing with a simple faith, we may yield ourselves unreservedly to Thy love, to be raised out of the depth of our misery by the depth of Thy mercy. Amen.

LXXVI.—Bishop Reginald Weber's Prayer for Conversion. Written in his book of Private Devotions, March 28, 1826, five days before his sudden death.

O my Father, my Master, my Saviour and my King, unworthy and wicked as I am, reject me not as a polluted vessel, but so quicken me by Thy Spirit from the death of sin that I may walk in newness of life before Thee. Convert me first, O Lord, that I may be the means, in Thy hand, of strengthening my brethren. Convert me, that I may be blessed to the conversion of many! Yea, convert me, O Jesus, for mine own sins' sake and the greatness of my undeserving before Thee, that I, who need Thy help most, may find it in most abundance. Lord, I believe, help Thou my unbelief! Lord, I repent, help Thou my impenitence! Turn Thou me, O Lord, and so I shall be turned.

Be favourable unto me, and I shall live. And let what remaineth of my life be spent in Thy service, Who liveth and reigneth with the Father and the Holy Ghost, now and for ever. Amen.

LXXVII.—Prayers from the Diary of the Rev. Richard Knill, of St. Petersburg, on the closing of an Old Year and the opening of a New Year. 1828—1829.

December 31, 1828. O my God and Father, all things concur to increase my debt of gratitude! By Thy grace I am what I am. Thy bounty feeds and clothes me, and every good and perfect gift cometh down from Thee. I feel, O Lord, that in everything I am deficient. I end the year lamenting over my cold and selfish heart, yet adoring Thy rich, free, and sovereign love. Hallelujah!

January 1, 1829. New Year's Day. The goodness of God to me is very great. Few among the human race have so much reason for gratitude. Lord, have mercy upon me, and help me to honour Thee! Let my services be acceptable in Thy sight, through Jesus Christ my Lord. Make this year peculiarly useful in the conversion of sinners; the increase of piety among true believers; the zeal of the Church; the circulation of the Holy

Scriptures and other good books, and the prosperity of all things connected with Thy cause. Oh! prosper the work of our hands upon us—the work of our hands, Lord, prosper Thou it!"

"Life of Richard Knill." By Charles M. Birrell. Page 149.

LXXVIII.—Prayer of Principal Forbes, of St. Andrew's. Written in his Journal on completing his twenty-first year. 1830.

. . . Make every branch of study which I may pursue strengthen my confidence in Thy overruling providence, that, undeceived by views of false philosophy, I may ever in singleness of heart elevate my mind from Thy works unto Thy divine essence. Keep from me a vain and overbearing spirit; let me ever have a thorough sense of my own ignorance and weakness, and keep me through all the troubles and trials of a transitory state, in body and soul, unto everlasting life, for Jesus Christ's sake. Amen.

LXXIX.—Another Prayer of Principal Forbes, on his return home after a protracted period of sickness and sorrow. SEPTEMBER, 1854.

O God, who hast visited us with many trials and led us, like the Israelites of old, from place to place, without any certain abode, bless, we beseech Thee, our return home, and mercifully grant that the afflictions and anxieties of that long probation may bear fruit in a more self-denying and godly life, and that we may have our hearts fixed on a yet more abiding resting-place, eternal in the heavens, for Jesus Christ's sake. Amen.

LXXX.—A Morning Family Prayer, by the Rev. Alexander Fletcher, D.D., of Finsbury Chapel, London. 1834.

["Fletcher's Prayers"* were once familiar in innumerable households throughout the country. They were contained in a portly volume, giving (1) The text of the selected portion of Scripture to be read, (2) "Reflections" on the same, (3) the Family Prayer. This was, in almost every instance, based upon the Scripture lesson read. We give a fair average specimen, the Reading being Gen. xxxii., Jacob at Peniel.

Fletcher called his "Guide to Family Devotion" "My Legacy to my Country and the Church of Christ."]

O Lord, who art the God of all grace and of all comfort, we would earnestly supplicate thy Spirit as a spirit of prayer at this time, that our hearts as well as our lips may be engaged in acts of holy devotion.

Thou art the Almighty Jehovah, and Thou dost mercifully exercise Thy power in preserving Thy people amid the dangers which assail them in their journey to their Father's house, while passing

* "A Guide to Family Devotion," by the Rev. Alex. Fletcher. George Virtue, 26, Ivy Lane. 1834.

through the vale of tears. Great was the danger to which Jacob, his family, and his property were exposed when his brother, burning with rage and revenge, came with four hundred men to destroy him. Thou didst avert the brother's rage, Thou didst change the storm into a calm. At Thy command, fraternal affection was enkindled in the bosom where malignant and resentful passion long reigned. O Lord, Thou savest by Thy right hand them who put their trust in Thee. Thou gavest to Thy servant the shield of Thy Salvation; Thy right hand did hold him up, and Thy gentleness did make him great.

For our multiplied and aggravated offences we deserve the severest chastisement and the heaviest judgments. In the midst of deserved wrath, O remember us with undeserved mercies. Thou delightest in mercy, and may we delight to seek mercy from Him who delights to bestow it. Sanctify to us the afflictions and trials of the past. May we see not only Thy justice but Thy wisdom and goodness in all that has befallen us. Jacob saw Thy goodness in all he suffered; O give us Jacob's faith, then shall we glorify Thee in the furnace and acknowledge that in mercy Thou hast afflicted us. Prepare us for the afflictions that are to come. Suffer us not to imagine that we are to escape them in the path of duty. Let the words of our Saviour ever be preserved alive in our remembrance, "Through much tribulation ye must enter the Kingdom." Blessed Jesus, give us Thy presence, counsel, and protection on our way to the Heavenly Canaan. As an host of angels met and defended Jacob, O give Thine angels charge over us, to hold us up in their hands.

Holy Spirit, impart Thy grace in the hour of temptation. When temptations are strong let faith be strong. The more the tempter strives, the more may we wrestle in prayer.

O teach the dear children to wrestle with God in prayer betimes, then they shall be preserved from ten thousand snares. All their days may they resemble wrestling Jacob.

We thank our God for the providential care of the last night, and that we are now prostrated before the throne of God, to supplicate the salvation which is in Christ. Lord save us: save us else we perish. Let Thy grace appear this day in our lives and conversation. Teach us to watch over ourselves, to watch as under Thine eye, and to watch as those who must give an account. In our worldly employments and in all we do, let a rich savour of unfeigned piety be constantly manifest. May it be evident that we have been with Jesus.

Forgive our sins and hear our imperfect prayers for a Saviour's sake. Amen.

LXXXI.—**A Family Morning Prayer, by Henry Thornton, M.P. (the Friend of William Wilberforce). Prepared for use in his own family.**

Almighty and Eternal God, our Creator and Preserver, and continual Benefactor, we desire to begin this day with the acknowledgment of Thy power and goodness, and of our obligation to love and serve Thee; and we beseech Thee to grant us grace to pass the whole of it in Thy fear, and in the fulfilment of Thy commandments.

Thou hast appointed to each of us our work in life. O Lord enable us diligently to perform our respective duties. Grant that we may not waste our time in unprofitableness or idleness; or be unfaithful to any trust committed to us, or put on the mere appearance of goodness, or endeavour in any respect to deceive those around us, but may we remember that Thine eye is upon us; and may we have the testimony of our consciences that, in simplicity and godly sincerity, we may have our conversation in the world. May truth be ever on our lips. May we be examples of all integrity and uprightness. Help us also to perform a kind and

Christian part towards those who may come under our influence. May we labour to do them service; and may we continually deny ourselves that we may the more effectually and abundantly minister to the various wants of others. May we rejoice with them that rejoice, and weep with them that weep, and be kindly affectioned one to another with brotherly love, in honour preferring one another.

We also beseech Thee to give us patience to bear the several trials and vicissitudes of life, with an equal and contented mind. Grant that we may not be perplexed with the cares of this world, or overwhelmed with unnecessary fears, but may we ever trust Thy gracious providence, and hope in Thy goodness and mercy.

Give to us, when we are in prosperity, a spirit of moderation and sobriety. Save us from pride and from self-indulgence. Deliver us from the love of earthly things, and teach us to remember that it is Thou who givest us all things richly to enjoy.

Bless unto us the afflictive circumstances through which we may pass. May we see Thine hand in all Thy various dispensations, and adore Thee for the several events of Thy providence, knowing that, if we truly love and serve Thee, all things will work together for our good

We commend to Thy fatherly care our friends and relations. Direct, O Lord, their steps in life and enrich them with all spiritual blessings in Christ Jesus. Vouchsafe unto them the pardon of their sins and the glorious hope of eternal life.

We pray for the rising generation. May they remember their Creator in the days of their youth, and find Thee to be their refuge in all the scenes through which they pass.

Have mercy on all who are in any sorrow or trouble. Do Thou provide for them through the riches of Thy grace and send special help in their hour of need.

Be favourable to this nation. Bless the Queen and all her Royal Family. Direct her counsellors. [Give wisdom to the Houses of Parliament.] Inspire the magistrates with integrity; and the clergy with the spirit of true religion. Deliver us from the hands of our enemies and give us peace among ourselves.

We offer up these our imperfect prayers in the name of Jesus Christ our Saviour. Amen.

From "Family Prayers." By the late Henry Thornton, Esq., M.P. 31st edition. Thomas Hatchard. 1854.

LXXXII.—*A Prayer. By James Russell Lowell.* 1841.

God! do not let my loved one die,
   But rather wait until the time
That I am grown in purity
   Enough to enter Thy pure clime.
Then take me, I will gladly go
So that my love remain below.

Oh! let her stay! She is by birth
   What I through death must learn to be:
We need her more on our poor earth
   Than Thou canst need in Heaven with Thee.
She hath her wings already, I
Must burst this earth-shell ere I fly.

Then, God, take me! We shall be near,
   More near than ever, each to each:
Her angel ears will find more clear
   My Heavenly than my earthly speech.
And still, as I draw nigh to Thee,
Her soul and mine shall closer be.

LXXXIII.—*A Prayer of the Abbé Lacordaire, when, at the commencement of his Station* of 1846, "on the morrow of the fiercest of all his struggles in the cause of liberty," he announced his intention of speaking on the familiar Life of Jesus Christ.* 1846.

Lord Jesus, during the ten years that I have been preaching to this audience, Thou wert ever at the bottom of my discourses; but to-day, at last,

---

* This word has a peculiar meaning in France. It is used to designate a series of sermons given annually by the same preacher, from the first Sunday in Advent until the Epiphany; and from the first Sunday of Lent until Low Sunday. These two periods are called *Stations*.

I come more directly to Thyself, to that Divine Face which is daily the object of my contemplation; to those Sacred Feet which I have so often kissed; to those loving Hands which have so often blessed me; to that Life whose fragrance I have inhaled from my cradle, which my boyhood denied, which my youth again learned to love, and which my manhood adores and preaches to every creature.

O Father! O Master! O Lover! O Jesus! help me more than ever, since, being nearer to Thee, my audience must feel it, and I must draw from my heart accents indicative of thy admirable proximity.

From "Memoir of the Abbé Lacordaire." By the Count de Montalembert.

LXXXIV.—**Evening Prayer for the Sick and Sorrowful. By Eliza Cook.** 1849.

> Let me ask Thee, ere I sleep,
> To remember those who weep,
> Those who moan with some wild sorrow,
> That shall dread to meet the morrow;
> Let me ask Thee to abide
> At the fainting sick one's side,
> Where the plaints of anguish rise
> In smother'd groans and weary sighs;
> Give them strength to brook and bear
> Trial pain, and trial care;
> Let them see Thy saving light;
> Be Thou " Watchman of their night!"

LXXXV.—**Prayer of Sir Robert Peel.** *Found in the private drawer of his dressing case, after his sudden death, July 2, 1850.*

Great and Merciful God, ruler of all nations, help me daily to repair to Thee for wisdom and grace suitable to the high office whereto Thy providence has called me. Strengthen, O Lord, my natural powers and faculties, that the weighty and solemn interests with which Thy servant is charged may not greatly suffer through weakness of body and confusion of mind. Deign, I beseech Thee, to obviate or correct the ill-effects of such omissions or mistakes in my proceedings as may result from partial knowledge, infirmity of judgment, or unfaithfulness in any with whom I may have to do. Let Thy blessing rest upon my Sovereign and my country. Dispose the hearts of all in high stations to adopt such measures as will preserve public order, foster industry, and alleviate distress. May true religion flourish, and peace be universal. Grant that, so far as may consist with human weakness, whatever is proposed by myself or others for the general good may be viewed with candour, and that all new and useful measures may be conducted to a prosperous issue. As for me, Thy servant, grant, O Merciful God, that I may not be so engrossed with public anxieties as that Thy word should become unfruitful in me, or be so moved by difficulty or opposition as not to pursue the narrow way which leadeth me to life. And, O most gracious Father, if, notwithstanding my present desires and purposes, I should forget Thee, do not Thou forget me, seeing that I entreat Thy constant remembrance and favour only for the sake of our most blessed Advocate and Redeemer Jesus Christ, to whom with Thee and the Holy Spirit be glory for ever. Amen.

LXXXVI.—*Prayer of Sir Henry Lawrence —" One who tried to do his duty." Written in his Journal amid the bustle of administrative work*, 2 October, 1852.

O Lord, give me grace and strength to do Thy will, to begin the day and to end it with prayer and searching of my own heart, and with reading of Thy Word. Make me to understand it, to understand Thee; to bring home to my heart the reality of Thy perfect Godhead and perfect humanity, and, above all, of my entire need of a Saviour; of my utter inability to do aught that is right in my own strength; make me humble, reasonable, contented, thankful, just, and considerate. Restrain my tongue and my thoughts; may I act as ever in Thy sight, as if I may die this day. May I not fear man nor man's opinions, but remember that Thou knowest my motives and my thoughts, and that Thou wilt be my Judge. It is not in me to be regular; let me be so as much as I can. Let me do to-day's work to-day, not postponing, clear up and finish daily; so living in humility, thankfulness, and contentment.

LXXXVII.—A Morning Prayer. By the Rev. E. B. Pusey, D.D. 1853.

[Dr. Pusey wrote many prayers for the private use of some members of his flock in whose spiritual history he was much interested. The following is a portion of one such prayer.]

O Eternal God, Author of my being, Fountain of all love, trusting in Thy love, I, a poor worm and miserable sinner, come before Thee to speak to Thee, to ask for Thy love. Thou knowest all I would ask Thee if I dared; Thou knowest how I would love Thee, if I could; Thou knowest all I would hope of Thee, if mine own unworthiness did not keep me back. Yet Thou givest me the longing, Thou wilt give what I long for, even Thyself. Thou preparest the heart—prepare my heart, O Loving God, that I may long for Thee more, adore Thee more humbly, ask at least with all the desires of my heart, all which Thou art ready to give me, if I love Thee. Make me to love Thee through all Thy love for me, through Thine own love in me.

O God, my God! I praise Thee and thank Thee

from my inmost heart that in all eternity Thou didst think of me and didst love me with Thine infinite love; that out of pure love for me Thou willedst to make me that I might love Thee and be loved by Thee, and be happy in Thy love. Thou willedst in all eternity to redeem me with the Precious Blood of Thine Only Co-equal Son; Thou willedst to unite me in Him to Thyself; Thou willedst that He should become man that we might, through Him, be one with Thee. This Thou willedst for me, too, O my God, and for this Thou didst wait for me when I looked not for Thee. Thou rememberedst me when I forgot Thee; Thou didst make me Thy child; Thou didst give me Thy graces; Thou didst speak to my heart; by all the yearnings of my heart Thou didst draw me unto Thee; if I did not hear Thee, Thou didst not weary, but didst anew call me, and Thou hast conquered and hast made me Thine. O then let my soul melt for love of Thee; let it melt through Thy love, into thy love, that in love I may adore Thee, in love serve Thee, in love thank Thee, in and with Thy love, love Thee everlastingly.

For these and all Thy blessings bestowed on me, Thy poor sinner, upon Thy whole Church, upon every member of Thy Church, and especially upon all whom Thou hast ever given me to love, or to be loved by me, for all the benefits of nature, providence, grace, up to this hour. . . . I give Thee most humble and hearty thanks in union with the thanksgivings of my Lord Jesus Christ, and of His whole Church in Heaven and in earth. Enlarge Thou my heart that I may love Thee more and more; kindle my soul that I may praise Thee; order my thoughts, words, and deeds that, within and without, I may be wholly Thine, wholly serve Thee, wholly praise and glorify Thee with all Thine Angels and Saints for ever and ever. . . .

And now, O God, I do desire this day most earnestly to please Thee; to do Thy will in each several thing which Thou shalt give me to do; to bear each thing which Thou shalt allow to befall me contrary to my will, meekly, humbly, patiently, persistently, as a precious gift from Thee to subdue self-will in me; and to make my will wholly Thine. What I do make me do simply as Thy child; let me be throughout the day as a child in his [her] loving Father's presence, ever looking up to Thee. If I joy, joying before Thee; if I sorrow, sorrowing unto Thee; if I work, working for Thee; if I rest, resting in Thee. May I breathe, think, speak, act, in Thy love. May I love Thee for all Thy love. May I thank Thee, if not in words yet in my heart, for each single gift of Thy love, for each refreshment of my body, for each comfort which Thou allowest me day by day. May I do nothing without looking to Thy grace, if not actually yet in the habit of my mind. Teach me how, momentarily, to ask Thee, silently, for Thy help. If I fail, teach me at once to ask Thee to forgive me. If I do anything ever so little well, teach me at once to thank Thee and own it all Thine. If I am disquieted enable me by Thy grace quickly to turn to Thee. O that with every breath I could tell Thee how I would love Thee; O that I could win others to Thy love; O that I could be perfected in Thy love; O that all my acts and words were penetrated, ensouled, transfigured with Thy love. May nothing this day come between Thee and me. May nothing for one moment separate me from Thee, or hide Thee from me. May I will, do, say just what Thou, my loving and tender Father, willest me to will, do, say; and may I not will, say, or do, whatever Thou, who so wisely and tenderly willest all things for my well-being and my salvation, willest me not to will, say, or do. . . .

Work Thy will in me and through me this day; protect me, guide me, bless me, within and without, that I may do something this day for love of Thee, though I see it not nor know it. Lead me, good Lord, in a straight way unto Thyself, and guide me by Thy grace unto the end through Jesus Christ my Lord and Saviour. Amen.

LXXXVIII.—*A Private Prayer, by John Sheppard, of Frome. For assurance as to not being wholly destitute of Christian Faith.* 1853.

O Thou who implantest and increasest faith, convince me, I beseech Thee, that my many prayers to Thee, and even this prayer which I now attempt to offer, must prove me to possess and exercise a *little* faith—even though it be but like an invisible seed, a spark, an atom; a little faith in Thee as the Omniscient, perfect, and forgiving God, reconciled in Thy dear Son and ready, through Him, to accept me. For, O my Lord, what a vain, hopeless, self-contradicting labour have all my prayers been, and this one like the rest, if I *dis*believe those facts, if I have *no* faith that Thou *art*, and art a rewarder of them that diligently seek Thee; no belief that Thou hearest, beholdest, understandest the thoughts which are addressed to Thee; no trust that Thou hast pity and kindness and acceptest those who humbly come to Thee in the way Thou hast revealed! O Lord, a *little* faith and hope in these things I must possess, though sometimes scarcely discernible, involved and obscured in doubts, suspicions, and misgivings.

Author of Nature, Giver of all Grace, Thou canst create, and augment, and multiply all things. Thou canst revive rapidly a feeble spark into a mighty flame. Thou canst unfold and nourish a latent atom into an organised life. Lord, increase my faith! Let it not fail and perish! O, Sun of Righteousness, Thyself develop it and make it to grow! Fortify and preserve it, O Lord, by Thy mercy, when the enemy comes in like a flood, and when my spirit faileth. Help me, though as with an enfeebled hand, to lay hold upon the Rock of my Salvation, or to touch the sceptre of Thy sovereign mercy. Let even my fears of Thy just displeasure assure me that I have some belief in Thy existence and perfections, and then permit me not to conceal from myself that glorious attribute of pardoning love, so clearly revealed in Thy Word; but do Thou graciously strengthen me to embrace, though it be with a *little* faith, the altar of atonement where that love was supremely manifested, and to feel that my redemption is complete in Him, whose lips often uttered, and whose death and triumph sealed, the precious promise—He that believeth on Me hath everlasting life. Amen.

From "Prayers chiefly adapted for Times and Occasions of Personal Trial." By John Sheppard. Jackson & Walford. 1853.

LXXXIX.—**Another Private Prayer by John Sheppard,** of **Frome. "For Pardon of Sin and Renewal of Heart under distressing Doubts."** 1853.

O Judge and Saviour of men, Thou knowest that with many temporal anxieties there is now combined the great paramount solicitude—have I truly an interest in Christ's divine redemption? Will He own me at last for His? The thought of multiplied sinfulness, after a long profession of attachment to His holy name, has caused the hope of this, at times, almost to die within me. I have felt as if I must at last be rejected from the number of His true followers; and, O my offended Lord, what a thought is this! What untold fears and ills does it involve! But must I then cease to pray? Must I renounce revealed hope, and give up my trust in the blood which cleanseth from all sin? Oh! if I have not known its true and vital application to my soul, not yet experienced its healing, purifying, new-creating power, visit me, I beseech Thee, with that divine and holy salvation! O pardon, now pardon me, through the peace-speaking blood of His cross who tasted death for every man; and save me, O Lord, from secret faults and from presumptuous sins! Deliver me from atheistic doubts, and from infatuation of heart! Impress a constant and deep sense of Thy holy presence on my spirit; pardon the countless instances in which grievous and tolerated evils dwelling in me have evinced that I had, for the time, no wakeful faith in Thy omniscient holiness, and in the misery of offending Thee!

O make *this* supplication genuine. Let it be the true, deep sighing of a contrite heart; and give me, I beseech Thee, a vital trust in Thy surpassing love manifested in the atoning blood of Jesus, shed for the remission of sins! Thou seest this heart full of evil tendencies, of unbelief, of worldliness, of fear, of selfishness, of doubt and disquiet. O touch and heal, pacify and strengthen it with Thy sovereign grace! Let this be the day of Thy power! Lamb of God, who takest away the sin of the world, grant me Thy peace! O speak forgiveness by the inward voice of Thy divine compassion! Display to my burdened soul that mighty and vast long-suffering which redeems and changes, restores and blesses, even when it seems too late! O take away the lurking distrust and doubt which are my bane, and pour a gleam of Heavenly consolation from Thy glorious gospel on Thy most unworthy worshipper! Increase my faith that I may far more deeply prize and venerate the one offering of the Lord Jesus Christ, and partake assuredly, although so unfaithful to this most affecting of gifts and claims, its sacred efficacy and power. Help me to feel its infinite value, and its sufficiency even for me!

Give an interest, good Lord, in this same unspeakable blessing to all that are dear to me, and unite us for ever, as ransomed transgressors, in Thy glorious kingdom, for our Mediator's sake. Amen.

XC.—**Dr. James Hinton on Prayer.** [*From a letter to a friend in religious difficulties.*] JANUARY, 1859.

"I think it was a letter of yours made me think of some things about prayer, which I never clearly recognised before, although they are very obvious when one sees them. There is a sort of feeling in our minds, as if there were no propriety in praying for a thing, if it is not *contingent,* as if a thing that was certain was excluded from its scope; and so to feel certain about things as being clearly promised or declared by God, was apt to make us feel an embarrassment in praying for them. I have felt this a good deal, but a little while ago it flashed upon me that there must be some radical misapprehension about prayer in my mind, for it is not at all that way that it is represented in Scripture. There, the representation of prayer is continually of it as being for things which are certain, and which are known and felt to be certain by those who pray. Just think of a few cases—one or two will do—and you will find it runs throughout the Scriptural representation of prayer. Thus, 'My heart's desire and *prayer to God* for Israel is that they might be saved'; and then he goes on 'So all Israel *shall be saved.*' And Paul, perpetually in his Epistles, prays for things he is sure will be—for blessings on the churches, *e.g.,* which he knows God will certainly give. So Solomon's prayer.

So the Lord's prayer. Is it not certain God's Kingdom shall come? But I think the most striking case is Christ's own prayers, which were for things He certainly knew should certainly be. Think of this a little.

Well, then, you see our notion of prayer, if we have such an one, as being inappropriate for that which is not doubtful, is quite unscriptural; and we must have a better one. Prayer does not mean the asking God for things we can't be sure about receiving if we don't pray. What it is I don't pretend to say I see, but this is a relief and blessing, surely, to know. It is something larger, higher, better than that, better than what we are apt to think of it. Surely this may do for us at the present, if it be all. Can we not let our spirits expand and flow into an *unknown* thought of prayer? When I try to think of it, as yet I don't get much further than Paul's words: 'We know not what to pray for as we ought, but the Spirit maketh intercession for us.' Do you know I incline to think that this presents the very truth of prayer for all times, and that we, and all who come after us in the flesh, will speak best of prayer when they say, 'I know not what to pray for as I ought, but something within me, which is above myself, speaks for me to God,' and especially of those things which He has promised, and on the assured belief on which all my life is based."

From "Life and Letters of James Hinton." By Ellice Hopkins.

XCI.—**Prayer used at the Meetings of the First London School Board.** 1870.

[Of this Board Lord Lawrence was Chairman. Among those who attended the prayer meeting of the Board were:—Samuel Morley, M.P., Canon Cromwell, Lord Lawrence, R. Freeman, Rev. J. Rodgers, John MacGregor (Rob Roy), Sir Charles Reed, M.P., T. B. Smithies, Rev. J.

A. Picton, J. Stiff, J. E. Tressider, A. McArthur, Prebendary Thorold (afterwards Bishop of Winchester), Dr. Joseph Angus, J. Watson, Very Rev. J. Mee, A. Lafone, J. B. Ingle, E. H. Currie, T. Scrutton, E. N. Buxton, W. H. Smith, M.P., Prebendary Barry, C. E. Mudie, H. S. Gover.]

Almighty and Everlasting God, who knowest the hearts of all men, and understandest all their ways, without whom nothing is strong, nothing is holy; Hear us, Thine unworthy servants, who now draw near to Thee, beseeching Thee to guide and prosper the work of our hands. May the dew of Thy blessing continually rest upon the whole of the wide field in which we are called to labour. As Thou hast taught us in everything, by prayer and supplication, with thanksgiving, to make known our requests unto Thee, do Thou impress upon us a sense of the solemn responsibility which rests upon us, and increase our faith in the assurance that Thou wilt direct those who, in all their ways, acknowledge Thee. Grant that we, and all associated with us in the great work of teaching and training the young and ignorant, may be so guided and overruled by Thee, in all our thoughts, words, and works, that the children entrusted to our care may learn in their early days to know Thee, the only true God, and Jesus Christ whom Thou hast sent.

Be present amid the deliberations of this day.

First London School Board. 1870.

Give us a constant sense of Thy presence. Vouchsafe to us the grace, the wisdom, the courage we may need. Direct and control all hearts, so that all things may be ordered and settled upon the best and surest foundations, and the children of this generation may become a people fearing Thee and working righteousness.

Guide with Thy counsels those who may be called to select teachers, and grant that there may never be wanting able and godly persons to carry forward the education of the children of this country. Bless the religious instruction given in the schools. May those who teach never be weary, amid the many discouragements of their work, in giving line upon line, precept upon precept; and may those who are taught have their hearts so opened by the Holy Spirit as to attend to the things spoken in Thy name from Thy word.

With these our prayers for future help and blessing, we join our praises and thanksgiving for what has been already done. We thank Thee that many, by means of the schools hitherto established, have been taught in childhood those Holy Scriptures which are able to make wise unto salvation through faith which is in Christ Jesus. Vouchsafe the continuance of Thy blessing to those who may come under instruction, granting them in this world knowledge of Thy truth, and in the world to come life everlasting, through Jesus Christ our Lord. Our Father, &c.

XCII.—*A Prayer by Miss Frances Power Cobbe. From "Alone to the Alone."* 1871.

O Lord our God, whose eye searchest for truth and purity of heart! Turn us now away from every vanity of thought, and draw forth some living light of trust and love, that we may meet Thee, spirit to Spirit, the weak to the Almighty, the sad and sinful to the only Blessed and Holy. O! Thou well-spring of eternal life! we bring to Thee the thirst we cannot quench; send the cooling drops which shall abate the fever of vain desire and baptise us with peace with Thee.

O! Thou Everpresent! there is no faithfulness gentle and long-suffering as Thine. All our unrest of soul cometh only hence, that we keep not close to Thee, nor lay ourselves freely open to Thy ready help. Thy calmness is ever by to swallow up our fretful cares; Thy silent looks to chide our eager words; Thy infinite purity to put to shame whatever is mean and low. Every hour of Eternity is full of Thee. There is no desert place in life or death where Thou art not. It is we alone, O Lord, that stray and change; and when our faithless spirits would return to Thee again, Thou stretchest forth Thine hand and comfortest us. Never may we forget Thee till sin hath made Thee terrible. Hold not Thy peace too long with us, O Thou All-Merciful! but chasten us betimes, ere we have ceased to lay Thy will to heart.

O Thou Eternal, in whose appointment our life standeth! Thou hast committed our work to us, and we would commit our cares to Thee. May we feel that we are not our own, and that Thou wilt heed our wants, while we are intent upon Thy will. May we never dwell carelessly or say in our hearts, "I am here and there is none over me"; nor anxiously, as though our path were hid; but with a mind simply fixed upon our trust, and choosing nothing but the dispositions of Thy Providence. Before Thee, O Lord, we have no rights, save to serve Thee with our toil and love Thee in our souls. Yet often have we coveted our rest before the time, and stretched forth our hand to gather it as the hasty fruit before the summer; and so it has been small and bitter to the taste. Henceforth, we would wait upon Thy seasons, and leave ourselves to Thee. More and more fill us with that pity for others' troubles which comes from forgetfulness of our own; with the charity of them that know their own unworthiness; with the alacrity of mortals that may not boast of the morrow, and the glad hope of the children of Eternity. Lead us in the straight paths of simplicity and sanctity; and may neither the flatteries nor the censures of men betray us into a devious step. And when the last dimness steals upon our eyes and draws the veil to hide all earthly light, give us to see, in the spirit, the gracious angels of Thy mercy to bear us from the scenes of time, and feel a spring of joys, permanent as the numbers of Eternity. And unto Thee, the Beginning and the End, Lord of the living, refuge of the dying, be thanks and praise for ever! Amen.

Quoted in "Home Prayers." By Dr. James Martineau. Longmans, Green & Co.

XCIII.—Prayer of the Prince Imperial of France. Written prior to his departure for Zululand, where he was slain, 1st June, 1879. Found, after his death, among his papers at Chislehurst, Kent.

My God I give to Thee my heart; but give to me faith. Without faith there is no strong prayer, and to pray is a longing of my soul. I pray, not that Thou shouldst take away the obstacles from my path, but that Thou mayest permit me to overcome them.

I pray, not that Thou shouldst disarm my enemies, but that Thou shouldst aid me to conquer myself. Hear, O God, my prayer; preserve to my affection those who are dear to me. Grant them happy days. If Thou givest on this earth a certain sum of joy, take, O God, my share and bestow it on the most worthy, and may the most worthy be my friends.

If Thou wouldst punish man, strike me. Misfortune is converted into happiness by the sweet thought that those whom we love are happy. Happiness is poisoned by the bitter thought that while I rejoice, those whom I love a thousand times better than myself, are suffering. For me, O God, no more happiness. Take it from my path. I can only find joy in forgetting the past. If I forget those who are no more, I shall be forgotten in my turn, and how sad the thought which makes one say, "Time effaces all." The only satisfaction I seek is that which lasts for ever, that which is given by a tranquil conscience.

O! my God, show me ever where my duty lies, and give me strength to accomplish it always. Arrived at the term of my life I shall then turn my gaze fearlessly to the past. Remembrance will not be for me a long remorse. Then shall I be happy.

Grant, O God, that my heart may be penetrated with the conviction that those whom I love, and who are dead, shall see all my actions. My life shall be worthy of their witness, and my inmost thoughts shall never make me blush.

XCIV.—Extempore Morning Prayer by Rev. C. H. Spurgeon. JUNE, 1878.

[Mr. Spurgeon was a believer in "miracles wrought by prayer," both in regard to spiritual and to temporal things. "I am constantly witnessing the most unmistakable instances of answers to prayer," he said on one occasion. "My whole life is made up of them. To me they are so familiar as to cease to excite my surprise; but to many they would, no doubt, seem marvellous. Why, I could no more doubt the efficacy of prayer than I could disbelieve the law of gravitation. The one is as much a fact as the other, constantly verified every day of my life. Elijah, by the brook Cherith, as he received his daily rations from the ravens, could hardly be a more likely subject for scepticism than I. Look at my Orphanage. To keep it going entails an annual expenditure of about £10,000. Only £1,400 is provided for by endowment. The remaining £8,000 comes to me regularly in answer to prayer. I do not know where I shall get it from day to day. I ask God for it and He sends it. Mr. Müller, of Bristol, does the same on a far larger scale, and his experience is the same as mine. The constant inflow of funds is not stimulated by advertisements, by begging-letters, by canvassing, or any of the usual modes of raising the wind. We ask God for the cash, and He sends it. That is a good, solid, material fact, not to be explained away."

The following prayer, uttered in the course of his usual pulpit ministrations, and taken down in shorthand, is a fair average specimen of Mr. Spurgeon's innumerable extempore prayers.]

Blessed God, our heart doth praise Thee, our inmost soul exults in Thy name, for the Lord is good, and His mercy endureth for ever. Thy people praise Thee, O God, for that Thou hast been unto them, and we can, each one, set forth Thy worthy praise by reason of our personal experience of Thy goodness. Thou hast dealt well with Thy servants, O Lord, according unto Thy Word. We bless Thee for teaching us from our youth, for some of us have known Thee even from childhood, and Thy Word was precious to us even in our earlier days when, like young Samuel, we were spoken to of the Lord. Now Thou hast borne and carried us these years in the wilderness with unchanging love and goodness, and there be some in Thy presence this morning who know that even to hoar hairs Thou art He. Thou hast made, and Thou dost carry; Thou dost not forsake the work of Thine own hands. Thy mercy endureth for ever, and let Thy praise endure for ever also.

O Lord, we would cling to Thee more firmly than we have ever done; we would say, "Return unto thy rest, O my soul, for the Lord hath dealt bountifully with thee; for Thou hast delivered my soul from death, mine eyes from tears, and my feet from falling." We would this morning "take the cup of salvation and call upon the name of the Lord." We would "pay our vows, now, in the courts of the Lord's house." Blessed be the name of the Lord we have been brought low, but the Lord hath helped us; we have oftentimes wandered, but He has restored us; we have been tried, but He has preserved us; yea, we have found His paths to be "paths of pleasantness," and all the ways of His wisdom to be "ways of peace." We bear our willing witness to the testimony of the Lord; we set our seal that "He is true," and we cry again, "Bind the sacrifice with cords, even with cords unto the horns of the altar." From henceforth let no man trouble us, for we "bear in our bodies the marks of the Lord Jesus." We are His branded servants henceforth and for ever. Our ear is nailed to our Master's doorpost, to go out no more for ever.

And now, Lord, we beseech Thee to hear the voice of our cry. Thy people would first of all ask Thee to deepen within them all the good works of Thy Grace. We do repent of sin; give us a deeper repentance. May we have a horror of it; may we dread the very approach of it; may we chastely flee from it and resolve, with sacred jealousy, that our hearts shall be for the Lord alone. We have faith in Jesus, Blessed be Thy name! but oh, strengthen and deepen that faith. May He be all in all to us; may we never look elsewhere for ground of rest, but abide in Him with an unwavering, immutable confidence that the Christ of God cannot fail nor be discouraged, but must for ever be the salvation of His people. We trust that we can say also that we love the Lord; but oh! that we loved Him more! Let this blessed flame feed on the very marrow of our bones. May the zeal of

Thine house consume us; may we feel that we love the Lord with all our heart, with all our mind, with all our soul, with all our strength, and hence may there be about our life a special consecration, an immovable dedication to the Lord alone.

O Lord Jesus, deepen in us our knowledge of Thee. Thou hast made the first lines of Thy likeness upon our character, go on with this work of Sacred Art till we shall be like Thee in all respects. We wish that we had greater power in private prayer, that we were oftener wrestling with the Covenant Angel. We would that the Word of God were more sweet to us, more intensely precious, that we had a deeper hunger and thirst after it. Oh, that our knowledge of the truth were more clear, and our grip of it more steadfast. Teach us, O Lord, to know the reason of the hope that is in us, and to be able to defend the faith against all comers. Plough deep in us, Great Lord, and let the roots of Thy grace strike into the roots of our being until it shall be no more "I that live," but "Christ that liveth in me!"

Holiness also of life we crave after. Grant that our speech, our thoughts, our actions, may all be holiness, and "holiness unto the Lord." We know that there be some that seek after moral virtue apart from God; let us not be of their kind, but may our desire be that everything may be done as unto the Lord, for Thou hast said, "Walk before Me and be thou perfect." Help us to do so; to have no master but our God; no law but His will; no delight but Himself. O, take these hearts, most glorious Lord, and keep them, for "out of them are the issues of life," and let us be the instruments in Thy hand, by daily vigilance, of keeping our hearts, lest in heart we go astray from the Lord our God. Until life's latest hour may we keep the sacred pledges of our early youth. We do remember when we were baptised into the sacred name. Oh, never may we dishonour that sacred ordinance by which we declared that we were dead to the world and buried with Christ. Some of us do remember our early covenant with God, when we made over to Him ourselves and all that we had. Oh, in life's last hour, when we bow ourselves for weakness, may it be to bless that sacred bond, and to "enter into the joy of our Lord." And, if Thou hast taught us anything since then, if Thou hast given us any virtue or any praise, may we hear Thee say, "Hold fast that which thou hast, that no man take Thy crown." Oh, let no brother or sister become distinguished in grace and then decline, let none bear fruit and afterwards become barren, but may our path "shine more and more unto the perfect day."

It is this our spirit craveth after with strong desire, that the whole of our life, from the commencement with Christ, to its ending with our being in Christ, may glorify and bring help to His Church.

And now hear Thou us again while we cry to Thee. Our chief desire is for Thy cause in the earth. We are often very heavy about it. The days seem to us to be neither dark nor light, but mingled. Oh! that the element of light may overcome the darkness! We do pray Thee, raise up in these days a race of men that shall know the Gospel and hold it fast. We do feel that we have so much superficial religion, so much profession without true possession to back it up. Oh Lord, may our churches be built with precious stones, and not with wood and hay and stubble. May we ourselves so know the Gospel that no one can beat us out of it; may we so hold it that our faces shall be like flints against the errors of the age; so practise it that our lives shall be an argument that none can answer for the power of the Gospel of Jesus. And with this be pleased to grant to Thy churches more power over the sons of men. Oh Lord, make Thy ministers throughout all the world to be more fruitful in soul-winning. Let us not rest without sowing the good seed beside all waters. Forgive us our coldness and indifference; forgive us that we sleep as do others, for it is high time for us to awake out of sleep! Oh Lord, do help us to live while we live: shake us clear of these cerements, these grave clothes, which cling to us. Say to us, most blessed Jesus, what Thou saidst concerning Lazarus of old, "Loose him and let him go!" May we get right away from the old death, and the old lethargy, and live under the best conditions of life—diligently serving God.

Help our dear brethren who stand far out in the thick heathen darkness, like lone sentinels; let them bear their witness well, and may the day come when the Christian Church shall become a Missionary Church, when all over the world those that love Christ shall be determined that He shall conquer. Thou hast not yet made the Church "terrible as an army with banners." Would God she were! May those days of Christian earnestness come to us, and then shall we look for the latter day of glory.

And now, Father, save any in this house that remain unconverted. May this day be the day of their salvation. We would most earnestly entreat that some word may drop into the most careless heart: and this prayer especially; convert this day, in this house of prayer, if it may please Thee, some that shall be very earnest Christians in years to come; take hold to-day on some whom Thou hast ordained to be like Paul, who shall be missionaries to the ends of the earth! Take hold of some that are specially set against Thee, some that are very bold spirits, even in sin—thorough-hearted in their wickedness. Convert such now! Say unto them, "See, I have made thee a chosen vessel to bear my name unto the Gentiles," and may there come such power with it, that they may not be disobedient unto the Heavenly vision. Thy Church needs such men! Oh, that such were brought out to-day! We put it up as a prayer to be registered in Heaven, and we mean to look for an answer, that Thou wouldst to-day take hold of some men that shall become afterwards leaders in the Church of God; this day striking them down with the sense of sin, and leading them to Christ.

The Lord bless our country. God save the Queen. Keep us in peace, we beseech Thee, and in times of congresses and deliberations* may there sit in the Council chamber One higher than the kings of the earth, and greater than the ambassadors thereof. Oh, that long-continued peace might happen to this poor earth, for its wounds are many. Behold how all things languish for the lack of peace. The Lord send it! Quicken trade and commerce, remove the

* Lord Beaconsfield left London on the previous day to attend the Berlin Conference.

complaining that is now heard in our streets; kindly consider us in the matter of the weather,* that the harvests may not be spoiled; and bless the people, O Lord. Let the people praise Thee, and "then shall the earth yield her increase."

The Lord grant all this with the forgiveness of sin, the acceptance of our person, and assist us ever to live to his glory, for Jesus' sake. Amen.

From "The Pastor in Prayer. Being a choice selection of C. H. Spurgeon's Sunday Morning Prayers." Elliot Stock. 1893.

XCV.—An Extempore Prayer by the Rev. Henry Ward Beecher. 1813—1887.

[Many of Ward Beecher's prayers were considered to be even more impressive than his sermons, full as they were of elevated thought expressed in fluent and appropriate words. One of his constant hearers, who caused a volume of his prayers to be written down in shorthand and published, said: "The continual diversity of the themes dwelt upon; the copiousness and beauty of the language, the evident absence of formality and pre-arrangement, with the graphic distinctness and completeness of the presentation, make these exercises worthy to be taken as models of extemporaneous prayer."

The main thought in the following prayer is, "God the only object of Trust."]

Thou art the Eternal God. Before Thee there is none else: no authority higher than Thine; no wisdom that is not borrowed from Thee. Thou art the centre and the source of existence, and we rejoice that we may believe, since in Thee we live and

* There was excessive heat in the metropolis; on the day when this prayer was offered there was a shade temperature of 91 degrees.

move and have our being, that Thou art full of goodness, that Love is Thy nature, that all Thine administration is for the purpose of infinite love.

We are not wandering in darkness and forgetfulness; we are not cast into the maze of confusions and undirected turmoils of life. Thou sittest regent: all things are naked and open before Thee, and Thou beholdest the end from the beginning. In Thy hand the most complex things are simple; the strangest things to our thought are plain to Thine. Thou wilt restrain the wrath of man, and cause the remainder of wrath to praise Thee, and the things that run adverse, all those causes which conflict in time, we shall behold them from the other side, and in the order of Eternity all things shall then appear wise, nothing fugitive, nothing erratic.

It is our joy that we may believe thus in Thee, O Thou God of our salvation, that art higher than all men, than princes, than kings. Thou art Thyself the Lord of Lords and the King of Kings. All things are beneath Thee, not that they may be trampled down, but that thou mayest look benignantly upon them from Thine infinite excellence, from the height of Thy glory, and conserve them. We believe that it is in Thine heart to bring forth unspeakable good, transcending far the measure of our thought or the tracing of our imagination. Nor do we desire to guide Thee by our thoughts, nor prescribe in our own feeling the way that Thou shouldst come. We simply desire to look up and adore—to believe, to trust, to love, to obey.

O Lord, when we look upon the face of things, and attempt to judge Thee by sight, how quickly are we rebuked by the darkness and confusion of our own minds—even the things most familiar to us deceive us; even the things most common are inexplicable. All the ways of life are convoluted; all the affairs of men are liable to such disasters and apparent minglings that we cannot understand the course of things. We read Thy providence in the history of nations with amazement; we behold the current affairs of life with awe and wonder; and if we were to establish our faith in the destiny of man, in the perfection of the race, in the growth of truth and purity, on that which has been and that which is, how should we falter at every step! We must live by faith and not by sight.

We rejoice that our God is so great that it is no impeachment of our wisdom to say that we cannot understand His ways. If Thou wert to be understood easily, then Thou wouldst be but little more than a man; and as Thou art the God of the Universe and the Father of Ages, and we desire to understand our relative place, and to know that Thou art moving upon the spheres of eternity and not upon the lines of this globe and of our eras of time, we desire to take Thee as the Lord God Almighty, comprehensive over all conception, endless, dateless. Before we can send back a thought, Thy government was supreme; from periods beyond our conception, Thou still wast the Eternal God; and to the end Thou shalt be for ever unfolding by Thy works what Thou art, for ever endlessly creating and sustaining and never exhausted.

And we desire, O Lord, to be so in sympathy with Thee that we may hold on for ever with Thee; though born of yesterday, never to die. We rejoice that we are to be Thy children and of Thy household, and that no disaster can come to us so long as Thou art supreme. "No weapon formed against thee shall prosper," Thou sayest unto Thy people, and we believe that it is so and shall be so; and while we cannot understand the history of Thy Church upon earth, nor fully comprehend the history of nations, nor understand the providences of the times in which we live, nor the influences that are operating upon human affairs, we do understand that Thy Kingdom shall be established in every heart; and that while there is confusion without, there may be peace within; and while we cannot understand Thee on the earth we can understand Thee in our own souls.

And now, we beseech Thee, that every one of us may attempt to build up the world, by building so much of it as lies in our own character, in our own development. May we feel that it is ours to put one more fair stone on the walls of Jerusalem on earth, and thus aid in perfecting this growing structure. May we, therefore, become more conscientious and equitable, more pure and moral, more truthful and truth-loving; may we be clothed with love as with a garment; may we have an active and vital sympathy with Thee; may we learn to discover Thy ways by a holy intuition. May we know what is right and what is wrong among disputed things; never seek to be less than that which is already believed to be right; but always strive to over-measure and rise to yet nobler conceptions of rectitude. May we make justice more just, purity more pure, and love yet more refined; and may we never seek to shield ourselves by excuses, nor to hide behind weaknesses, and variously explain delinquencies.

We pray that Thou wilt remember every one of Thy people before Thee, in their special and common wants. Be near to those who are passing the last days of their lives upon earth, that are glorifying

God with the going down of the sun. Let them compose their minds with peace and with joy, and grant that they may, by anticipation, take hold of the rest that remaineth for the people of God; and we pray that their testimony and example and encouragement to the young may be such as to make them evermore examples and leaders in the host of God.

Remember those upon whom are the burdens of life. O! make them rest who carry the yoke, and those who are in the midst of suffering and who from day to day are vehemently exercised with various duties, may they be strong in the Lord, diligent in business, fervent in spirit, serving the Lord. May they learn how to serve Thee by their family duties; may they know how to look upon their secular affairs as a part of that which God requires at their hand; and may they be, in the discharge of these things, so imbued with justice, with truth, and with love, that it shall be a perpetual religious service. Thus may they never have occasion to pass from the sanctuary to the world, but may the world itself become their sanctuary, and their altar everywhere, with their God for ever present with them.

We beseech Thee that Thou wilt look upon those that are growing up into life and are beginning now to take hold upon manhood. O! let them make no fatal missteps, lest they be dashed in pieces from the very beginning; let them not listen to false teachings; especially may they not listen to their guilty passions, or be misled as to faith and truth by the suggestion of corrupt hearts; but may they, from the morning of life, be consecrated in all truth and honour to the cause of Jesus Christ. May they take care of each other, and may the young care for the young. Bless, we beseech Thee, our children. Thou hast made us to know many things by reason of them; they have taught us more than ever we have taught them.

We thank Thee that thus Thou hast opened our hearts to know the great things out of Thy law of love; that Thy Word has its perpetual ministry in our households, and that Thou hast united us together as husbands and wives, parents and children —that in our own daily visible experience we might understand the Word of God to us, who are the children of God—of God who is the Father of every living creature. We pray Thee to help us to rear our children as God would rear us, teaching and taught, receiving from them much by their silent example, and yielding much to them by our own example. May we be faithful to our trust: may we not be misled to weakness through over-fondness of affection for them, but may our love be chastened; may we learn to take them in the light of the eternal world, and behold their immortality even in their infancy.

Sanctify the family; and grant, we beseech of Thee, that it may be a gate of Heaven to every one of us. Bless us in our association one with another; may we have more and more noble conceptions of the relations of friendship. May we every day cleanse and purify ourselves from all the vulgarities, from all the selfishness, and from all the meanness to which we are liable by our contact with this world. May we get higher conceptions than those which we have of duty one toward another, and of all the duties of affection and of true friendship. May there spring from the heart of Christ in the heart of every one of His children, more and more nobility of purpose, more and more heroism of conception, more and more manliness of life.

Are there any that are looking wistfully into this sanctuary? Are there any that do not believe the things that make us supremely joyful? Oh, Lord, we beseech Thee, that they may understand, not by the power of reflection, but may they be taught that true wisdom is in experience, and may they seek the things that are pure as God interprets purity—things that are wise, as Thou dost interpret wisdom—things that are generous, noble, and good; and from some experience in these things may they begin to learn their truth, and so, through the realisations of love, may they come to the conceptions of truth.

And we beseech Thee that Thou wilt fulfil Thy kind designs and purposes toward all mankind, hastening the day when men shall have their reason so high that they may cast off prejudice and selfishness and all that is hateful and divisive, and may all on earth begin to find the drawings of love; and all men begin to help mankind. May all the earth begin to bear witness that God is coming in His final power to give ripeness to the race; and may all things that are offensive and selfish, and proud, and hateful, and cruel, begin to sink in power, and all things that are refined in wisdom, goodness, love, and purity, begin to gain front and strength.

O! hasten, Thou that from on high art the God of battles—not of clashing battles of steel and iron, but Thou that dost contend in the heavens, and upon the earth, and round about the universe, in that great and universal conflict between good and evil—make haste that the final glory be consummated, that the earth may rest as a ship long tempest-tossed and not comforted—rest when at length it finds its peaceful harbour. O bring this world at last to the bosom of Christ, and there may it find that anchorage and peace which it has so long sought in vain in its course. And all the glory of this victory, and all the glory of our own salvation therein, we will give to the Father, the Son, and the Holy Spirit. Amen.

XCVI.—*A Prayer for the Last Evening of the Year.* By J. Oswald Dykes, D.D. 1881.

Jehovah, God of Israel, who art from everlasting to everlasting; a thousand years are in Thy sight as yesterday when it passed. Before Thee the tribes of men are borne away as with a flood; they pass like a watch in the night and are gone. For we dwell in a house of clay. Few and evil are the days of the years of our pilgrimage. We are strangers and sojourners with Thee, as all our fathers were.

In Thine own hand, O Almighty Creator, hast Thou reserved the times and seasons which Thou hast allotted to the children of men, and we adore thy sovereign goodness in sparing us until this day. We praise Thee for permitting us to close, this evening, another year of life, and we thank Thee that goodness and mercy have followed us thus far upon our way. Thou hast been our Shepherd, and we have not wanted. Through the promise of the spring, the brightness of the summer, and the riches of the autumn, Thou hast been a ceaseless Benefactor unto us. Our souls look back with gratitude along the path by which we have been led. Alike in sunshine and in cloud, Thy hand hath upheld, Thy bounty hath blessed us.

We confess, O Lord, that we have failed to improve as we might have done, and ought to have done, the discipline of the year that is dying. Its opportunities for usefulness have often fled past, unemployed. Much of its daily work has been performed with negligent hand. We regret our wasted leisure, the needless pain we have sometimes caused, and the undevout spirit in which we have spent our days. In wonderful forbearance hast Thou borne with Thine undeserving children; chiding only in gentle tones, and waiting long upon our amending.

O God, we humbly ask forgiveness this night for all that is past. And, as we sadly remember how short our time is like to be, we beg for grace to use it better. May we redeem our days from vain conversation and gather up each fragment of time that nothing be lost. May we improve well our several talents and prepare ourselves for the day of final reckoning. Impress us deeply, O Lord, with the solemnity of living, the certainty of dying, and the nearness of judgment, and grant that we may so number our days, and ponder our latter end that we may all of us apply our hearts to heavenly wisdom.

Most gracious Saviour, we pray Thee earnestly to take each one of our family into Thy favour, and knit our souls to Thee by living faith and lowly love. Forbid it, Lord, that so much as a single member of this household should close this year a stranger to Thy grace.

Extend Thy mercy, we beseech Thee, to all we love. Have in Thy holy keeping throughout this night our kindred and our friends; and grant that, dwelling safely beneath Thy wing, they may enjoy, in the new year about to dawn, every earthly with every spiritual blessing. Let the troubles of each past season be forgotten in the joys that are yet to come, and let the years of time be for them, and for all of us, a fitting preparation for that everlasting day which hath no night.

Be pleased, O Father of Mercies, to relieve every one who closes the year in penury or danger, in distress of mind, or anguish of body. Upon all the children of affliction let the new day dawn with hope and healing in its wings. Through the unknown changes of our future, cause us to abide under the defence of the Most High, so shall no evil happen unto us. With long life do Thou satisfy us and show us Thy salvation, so shall we dwell in the house of the Lord for ever. Amen.

From "Daily Prayers for the Household." By J. Oswald Dykes, D.D. Nisbet & Co., Limited.

XCVII.—Prayers of the Seventh Earl of Shaftesbury, K.G. D. 1885.

[Lord Shaftesbury, the great philanthropist, was a "man of prayer." Throughout his exhaustive diaries there are hundreds of brief, comprehensive, prayers bearing upon the subjects recorded for the day. He had learned to "pray without ceasing"; prayer had become to him a natural habit of the mind; every task he undertook was begun, continued, and ended in prayer. A few specimens—the burden of a sigh, the falling of a tear, the upward glancing of the eye when none but God was near—will indicate the nature of his inner life and the terms in which he spoke with God.]

For Factory Labourers in their struggle (1841) for Just Legislation.

O God, the God of all righteousness, mercy, and love, give us all grace and strength to conceive and execute whatever may be for Thine honour and their welfare, that we may become at last, through the merits and intercession of our common Redeemer, a great and a happy, because a wise and understanding people.

Before an important Speech on the Mines and Collieries Bill. 1842.

["As I stood at the table," wrote Lord Shaftesbury, "and just before I opened my mouth, the words of God came forcibly to my mind, 'Only be strong and of a good courage.' Praised be His Holy Name, I was as easy from that moment as though I had been sitting in an arm-chair."]

Grant, oh blessed God, that I may not be exalted above measure, but that I may ever creep close by the ground, knowing and joyfully confessing that I am Thy servant, that without Thee I am nothing worth, and that from Thee alone cometh all counsel, wisdom, and understanding, for the sake of our most dear and only Saviour, God manifest in the flesh, our Lord Jesus Christ! . . . God prosper the issue!

Before a Motion on the Opium Question. 1843.

Alas what a weak faith I have! I have never yet failed of God's aid and favour, and yet I am ever in doubt and difficulty. Lord, I believe, help Thou my unbelief . . . Oh, God, be Thou with me in the hour of trial; speak to me the words that Thou spakest to Thy servant Joshua, and touch my lips, like Isaiah's, with fire of the altar—but take to Thyself all the glory, blessed Lord in Jesus Christ our Redeemer.

On bidding Farewell to Ragged School Boys Emigrating to Australia. 1848.

["... Gave a tea party to take leave of our 'ragged' emigrants to Australia, ragged no longer, thank God! ... It was a deeply religious meeting, and a feeling of piety and gratitude pervaded us all."]

And now, here as then, I commit them, oh Lord! to the word of Thy grace—prosper the work! bear them safely, happily, joyously, to their journey's end! Watch over them in body and in soul: make them Thy servants in this life and Thy saints in the next, in the mediation and everlasting love of Christ, our only Saviour and Redeemer!

For Abolition of the Slave Trade. 1852.

[November 18th, 1852. "An anti-abolition party has triumphed, and has elected a kindred President in the United States ... May not the extremity of the bondage be, as in the case of the Israelites, the moment of deliverance?"]

Oh, Lord, hear our prayer; Christ Jesus hear our prayer, and maintain thine own word of mercy, truth and peace! Have pity on our ignorance and infirmity, and make us to understand why it is that such special and singular horrors, in every form of physical and moral sin, are thus long permitted.

At the Outbreak of the Indian Mutiny. 1857.

August 29, 1857.—Number and variety of things to be prayed for: That He will quell the mutiny and give us a speedy victory; that He will make this outbreak the commencement of a new order of things; of a wiser and more vigorous government; of justice and judgment; of greater knowledge and greater zeal for man's real good; of fresh openings for the advance of the gospel; of enlarged missionary operations; of increased opportunity to promote and invite the Second Advent.

That He will protect, shelter, and deliver from their unspeakably ferocious enemies, the helpless women and children outraged, tortured, murdered, by the incarnate fiends of Hindostan.

That He will abate the sufferings of our troops already in the field, supply their wants, give them repose, sustain their courage; that He will hide, in the hollow of His hand, those now going out to India, and console the wives, the mothers, the children that are left behind in sorrow and anxiety.

XCVIII.—A General Prayer for Public Worship. By John Service, D.D., Minister of Wyndland Established Church, Glasgow. 1885.

[It was the custom of Dr. Service to write his prayers with great care and thought, endeavouring to express the spiritual aspirations of the whole congregation. In their delivery he did not confine himself to any one of his written prayers, but selected portions from various prayers according to the necessities and requirements of the occasion.]

Almighty God, whom no man hath seen, but who art everywhere present, and, in this sinful world, present always, to bless and save; to Thee shall all flesh come. Thou givest us rest this day from common work and toil; from our ordinary occupations and week-day cares, and we desire to come unto Thee as children unto a father, that we may enjoy here, in Thy house, a higher and fuller sense of Thy presence and grace than is common in our common lives. The Lord is nigh unto all that call upon Him, to all that call upon Him in truth; He will also hear their cry and will save them. We are sure that Thou wilt hear us; sure, also, that what is best for us Thou wilt freely give us. Grant, Lord, that we may desire, above all, not Thy gifts, but Thyself, and may seek Thy face, with all our hearts.

Father, who hast made the world beautiful, and hast given us faculties and powers to enjoy its beauty, we know that Thou art Thyself more to be desired than all Thy works. None of them, nor all of them, satisfy us or fill up the measure of our desires and hopes. In the enjoyment of them, and much more in the midst of changes which affect them, we are filled with a sense of vanity, and disappointment, and unrest. Thou alone, infinite and eternal Righteousness and Love, art our portion and inheritance. To Thee shall all flesh come. O Thou that hast breathed a spirit into man, and hast given us understanding and knowledge, in Thee, and in Thee alone, can we find rest for our souls. O satisfy us early with Thy mercy, and show us Thy salvation.

There is forgiveness with Thee, O Lord, that Thou mayest be feared, and plenteousness of mercy that Thou mayest be sought unto. We come to Thee and seek Thy face that our sins, which are many, may be forgiven us, and that even as sin hath abounded in us, grace may much more abound. O Thou who preventeth us with the blessings of goodness, and extendest Thy mercy when it is not welcomed or desired, who art kind even to the evil and unthankful, we do not need to entreat Thee to pardon us, but, we beseech Thee, enable us by Thy grace truly to repent of our sins, so that Thy pardon may cleanse, and Thy redemption save us. We remember before Thee this day, when we seek Thy presence, our past lives, how full they have been of mercies and benefits, and how empty of gratitude and of good deeds; how much we have received and how little we have given; in how many ways we have been taught of Thee and how little we have learned except folly; how many opportunities we have had to become purer and better, and wiser and happier, and how little we have profited by them, how many of them we have not used at all. We recall to mind how much our religion has been a name, our worship a form, our duty a hard task, our life a vain show; we remember how fondly we have clung to earthly pleasures and satisfactions, and how dull has been our sense of the beauty of holiness and the divinity of goodness. We remember, and we confess, how like our lives have been to those of the vain multitude, without God and without hope in the world, and how unlike the life of Him who, to save us by His example, was holy and harmless and undefiled and separate from sinners. We remember these our sins; we desire to remember them with a godly sorrow. Lord be merciful to us, and from all our hardness of heart and from all our unbelief and vanity and earthliness, be pleased to deliver us.

We thank Thee for Thy unending benefits and Thy boundless pity. Day and night alike declare Thy glory and, in our lives, the light and the darkness, prosperity and adversity, joy and sorrow, are witnesses of Thy love. We bless Thee that while sin and folly and ignorance and superstition, and all the evils of which men are guilty, and by which they are oppressed, are temporary in their nature, Thou Thyself, infinite in goodness, boundless in mercy and truth, art for ever light in the midst of darkness, order and beauty in the midst of all trouble and confusion. We thank Thee that out of seeming evil Thou still bringest forth good, and that as the rains from heaven water the earth, and return not whence they came without effect, so all Thy dealings with our race tend to the coming of Thy kingdom and the prevalence of righteousness and truth. We thank Thee for the good which befell men in past times, and which we inherit from them. We bless Thee that in our days we see how evils of past times have, by Thy care and providence, been turned to good. Our fathers suffered not in vain for themselves or us, but what they sowed in tears we reap in joy. Great and good men lived and toiled in past ages, and we have entered into their labours. For the best who live now, for Thy chosen servants in this generation, and in all generations to come, the common work and toil and suffering of common men have stored the world with good. We bless Thee, Lord of all, that Thy glory and our good are still the same, and that Thou art great and that Thy kingdom and glory shall have no end.

We bless Thee, Lord, for health; for the comforts of home; for the joys of kindred and acquaintance;

for all the unnumbered mercies with which our lot is enriched and blessed. We thank Thee for ability to work and earn our daily bread by daily toil; for toil which makes rest sweet, and rest which refreshes us for toil; for the varied experience of human life and its progress from youth to age. We thank Thee for the rain and the sunshine which, in their season, cause the earth to bring forth, and for the constant influences of goodness by which summer and winter, seed-time and harvest, keep their unfailing order and yield us their unfailing treasures.

We bless Thee and praise Thee, above all, for what Thou hast done for us, and in us, in giving us reasonable souls and revealing to them, through Jesus Christ, Thine own eternal grace and glory. We know in part and prophesy in part, and see through a glass darkly, but we bless Thee that we know that Thou art, and that Thou art the Rewarder of them that diligently seek Thee, rich in mercy to all that call upon Thee. Blessed be Thy name we are not left alone in this world of mystery, but have Thee beside us, a light to lighten our darkness, an almighty arm on which to lean in weakness, a very present help in trouble. We thank Thee for Jesus Christ, for the nearness with which we have been brought to Thee in Him, for the new and living way into Thy presence which

He has opened for us, for that newness of life which comes to us through Him, and that eternal life which is by Him to as many as believe in His name.

Grant, blessed Lord, that, having these gifts and benefits, we may live to show forth Thy praise, living not unto ourselves but unto Thee. It is Thy world in which we live, may we work Thy work while we are in it. It is Thy bounty that nourishes our life, may we dedicate our life wholly to Thee. May we so live that every day, according to Thy will, we may grow wiser and better and nobler, more full of the spirit of charity and brotherliness, and more free from envy and guile and greed. Every day may we seek to learn some new truth, to gain some new view of Thy glory and Thy grace, and to attain some new virtue and nobleness.

While all things in heaven, and in earth, and in our mortal bodies, change from day to day, may there be increased in our souls the righteousness of Christ, so that when the earthly house of our tabernacle is dissolved we may have a building of God, a house not made with hands, eternal in the Heavens. Amen.

From "Prayers for Public Worship." By the late John Service, D.D. Macmillan. 1885.

XCIX.—**Prayer at the Burial of the Dead. By John Serbice, D.D., of Glasgow.**

The Lord is merciful and gracious.

O Thou, who art the Beginning and the End of all lives, in whom the living live and the dead sleep, grant that we, in the presence of death, may feel that our true life is in Thee. Thou hast made us as we are made, to love life, and to grieve and suffer in the presence of death; be near to us when we call upon Thy name, feeling in that presence we have no help save in Thee alone.

It is our comfort and consolation in turning our hearts to Thee, when they are made heavy by sorrow, that Thou art greater than our hearts and knowest all things; that our grief, when it is too great to be uttered, and our need, when it is more and deeper than we know or can express, is what Thou knowest altogether. If, Lord, it seems to us when we need Thee most, and Thy help is most to be desired for our relief, that Thou art farthest away from us, and we are most left to ourselves; if the burden of life has thus, through our weakness, to be borne by us often without that help which it is Thine to give, do Thou, most Merciful, have compassion upon us, be near to us to keep us, even when we have not strength to call upon Thy name.

It is Thy hand, Father Almighty, which has fashioned the ties that bind us one to another in love and friendship, and when these ties are broken by death, that which we have to suffer is known to Thee and Thee alone. May we come to Thee as children unto a father, asking from Thee for a childlike confidence to make our requests known unto Thee, remembering that like as a father pitieth his children so the Lord pitieth them that fear Him. We desire to feel, though we cannot know, that Thy will in trouble and affliction, even the greatest of all, is not to punish us but to bless us; that alike in all that we are born to suffer in our affections, and in all the happiness and enjoyment that we derive from them, the pity and goodness of the Highest are manifested and expressed. When we shrink, as we do now, from the painful part of the discipline of this life, when our grief is heavier than we can bear, when all that is best and sweetest in the gift of life is withdrawn from it by Him who gave it, when our strength is proved to us to be weakness, in our weakness be Thy strength perfected, and may we lean upon it and feel that Thou art a very present help in trouble. We desire in our darkest hours to trust Thee, and against doubts and fears that test us and perplex us, to cling to the belief that all is for the best, not meant to crush us or to extinguish our hopes and desires for those we love and for ourselves, but to work out, for them and for us, good beyond our belief and hope.

When our faith is weak, and heart and flesh faint and fail, good Lord have mercy upon us; in Thy mercy remember us, inclining us to remember Thy mercy; in Thy pity visit us, that in the thought of Thy pity we may be saved from despair of ourselves. Most Merciful Father, seen of no creature Thou hast made, but near to all that live, and in all that lives, we, who see Thee not, and dimly reason of Thy existence and Thy ways, are made subject to doubt and fear in being made subject to death and the sorrow which is by death. Thou knowest how hard it is for us to assure ourselves, when those we love better than life are taken from us, that we are not forgotten or disowned by Him that made us; that our loss is not all loss, and our suffering and anguish not all vain and fruitless. Our affections cling to that which is earthly and familiar to us, so that it is hard for us to think and feel that our beloved dead, whose faces we shall no more behold, are still with Thee, and that for Thee, and in Thy presence and Thy dominion, death hath no more dominion over them.

Lord have mercy upon us, and when our faith is thus weak and faltering, increase our faith. When the witness of Thyself which Thou hast given to men is most precious and most needful, may we seek it and find it not only in the experience of Thy saints and servants in past ages, but in our own hearts, fashioned by Thee, and in our own lives, ordered by Thee. Like as a father pitieth his children, even so the Lord pitieth them that fear him. Even as we are moved by pity for the weak and downcast and sorrowful so our hearts assure us it must be that He, who is the Highest of all, must be the best of all, pitiful and compassionate beyond our belief and hope to all that lives and breathes.

Grant, our Father, that we may in all trouble that is darkest and deepest, find, in this revelation of Thyself within us, Thy consolation ministered to us, and Thy light lightening our darkness. . . . .

From "Prayers for Public Worship." By the late John Service, D.D., Glasgow. Macmillan. 1885.

C.—Prayer by Dr. Joseph Parker (of the City Temple). 1889. [Scripture Reading, Ps. xlii.]

Almighty God, our souls long for Thee, for Thou only canst satisfy our hunger and heal our sorrows. We are alone when Thou art absent, but when Thou art near our loneliness is turned into a great and tender joy. That Thou mayst be near to us evermore is our heart's highest desire. We will speak aloud of Thy goodness, for it is rich and continual; and we will tell of Thy mercy, for it is tender beyond all other pity. We cannot speak of ourselves as other than unworthy. We are, indeed, witnesses against ourselves. Lord, have mercy upon us; Christ, have mercy upon us. Father of our souls, wash us in the precious and all-cleansing blood of Christ.

Behold, Thou dost work a daily miracle in our daily preservation; yea, Thou dost create us again in every breath we draw. Our life is hidden from us so that we cannot see it; it is in us, but we may not look upon it; it throbs in our heart, but it may not be touched by our hand. How can we redeem it, or how can we save it from death? Truly salvation is of the Lord alone, and the redemption of our life is the work of the Most High. Unto Him that loved us, and hath washed us from our sins in His own blood, unto Him be glory evermore.

Giver of all Good, give us what we need day by day while life shall last. Make our habitation as one of Thy sanctuaries; turn our tears into unexpected joys; make us the better for our afflictions and richer for our losses; hide Thy secret in our heart that we may have bread to eat that the world knowest not of, and pour Thy blessing upon our whole life. O Lord, hear us. Blessed

One, let our prayer come back again in sweet replies of love. Father of all grace, everlasting Son of God, Holy Ghost the Comforter, save us now, and save us evermore. Amen.

<small>From the "People's Family Prayer Book," No. cxlviii. By Joseph Parker, D.D. Simpkin, Marshall & Co., Limited.</small>

CI.—**Another Prayer by Dr. Joseph Parker.** 1889. [Scripture Reading, Ps. civ. 1—24.]

Almighty God, all the light is Thine. We pray Thee that we may walk in the light; and know how near Thou art, and feel the touch of Thy hand; then all shall be brightness and joy; yea, then shall be in our hearts a whole heaven of peace, and whilst we are yet on the earth we shall be in the society of the spirits of the blessed. Thou hast made ours a wondrous life; we cannot tell what it is, in all its mysteries of pain, and love, and fear, and hope. Verily, we are fearfully and wonderfully made. We would know whence we are, why we are here, whither we are going; we seem to be breathing questions continually to Heaven, and yet how seldom do we hear replies. Yet Thou dost answer us, in new impulse, in purified motive, in an outgoing of soul which Thou alone couldst create and sustain. Great is the mystery of godliness—all godliness, all good conduct, all sweet temper, all heavenly charity. Oh that we might know more of this mystery, and exemplify our knowledge in behaviour such as becometh saints. Yet Thou knowest our frame, Thou rememberest that we are dust; Thou art pitiful towards us,—yea, our infirmities are our plea. Our life is a great cry of need, often a sharp utterance of pain, always a great wonder and a sacred hope.

Spirit of the living God, come now—Spirit of fire, answer us from the high heavens—Spirit of life, let Thine answer be unto us great and tender and full of satisfaction. Dry the tears of our sorrow, lift us up when we are cast down, speak comfortably unto us, let tender solaces recover our strength, and messages from heaven rekindle the lamp of our hope. Oh save us, Mighty One—draw us to Thyself, and set not the foot of Thy power upon any one of us, or we shall be destroyed, but open Thine heart and bid us welcome to Thy love, and show us the meaning of the Cross. Amen.

From the "People's Family Prayer Book," No. clxxxix. By Joseph Parker, D.D. Simpkin, Marshall & Co., Limited.

CII.—Prayers by Professor W. Gray Elmslie, D.D. 1848—1889. [Hitherto unpublished.]

["Although Dr. Elmslie was not destined to a long career, and died with the greater purposes of his life-work almost entirely unfulfilled, very few men in the Nonconformist Churches of Great Britain were better known and loved. The expectation of many in his native Scotland were fixed on him from the first; in England no preacher of his years had a larger or more enthusiastic following."—*Dr. W. Robertson Nicoll.*

Among Dr. Elmslie's last words were these: "No man can deny that I always preached the love of God. That was right, I am glad I did not puzzle poor sorrowful humanity with abstruse doctrines, but always tried to win them to Christ by preaching a God of Love."]

General.

O God, the Father of Lights, from whom cometh down every good and perfect gift, we bring to Thee the offering of our praise and prayer in return for all the mercies of the week gone by [or, of this day].

We bless Thee for the gift of life, and for all those things that make it beautiful and good. We praise Thee for health of body and soundness of mind, for protection from harm and strength for toil, for food and warmth and the comfort of a home, for the parents and teachers and benefactors of byegone days, for faithful servants, for kind neighbours and loving friends, and for all who by word or deed are helping us to bear the burden of life, and cheering us on our homeward way.

Above all, we thank Thee for the knowledge of our redemption through Jesus Christ, for the presence in our hearts of His Holy Spirit, for the assurance of succour and support amid the trials of life, and for the hope of a blessed immortality in the world to come.

We desire, O Lord, with humbled hearts to acknowledge Thy great pitifulness and patient forbearance towards us who so often and so deeply offend Thee by the wilfulness and waywardness of our thoughts, words, and deeds. Each day of our life we grieve Thee, far more than we can know or understand, by our want of thought and lack of love, by misuse of mercies and forgetfulness of Thee the giver, by anxious cares and needless fears, or by foolish repining and thankless discontent, by excessive engrossment in earthly concerns, by unworthy thoughts and forbidden acts, and by countless failures of faith and love towards God and towards men. For these, and all other sins that we have done wittingly and unwittingly, we crave forgiveness, and pray for grace that we may prove our penitence and show forth our gratitude by a greater goodness to our fellow men, a more constant remembrance of Christ, our Master, and a closer walk with God.

We beseech Thee, O Lord, for all the sinful and sorrowful sons of men in their manifold troubles and temptations, and for all good men and women who are striving to alleviate their sorrow and to save them from their sins. We remember with compassion the sick and poor and homeless, the widow and orphan, the outcast and fallen and tempted, the careworn and weary and despairing, the lonely and bereaved. We pray for the downtrodden and enslaved, for the wronged and oppressed, for those who wander in the darkness of heathendom, and for all who, with breaking hearts, grope vainly amid doubt and error for the light of God's love that shines for us from the face of Jesus Christ. O God,* of unchangeable power and eternal light, look favourably, we beseech Thee, on the whole Church of Christ, set as a light from Heaven in this dark world of ours, and, by the tranquil operation of Thy perpetual providence, carry out the work of man's salvation and let the whole world feel, and see, that things which were cast down are being raised up, and things which had grown old are being made new, and all things are returning to perfection through Him from whom they took their origin, even through our Lord Jesus Christ. Amen.

[If the foregoing prayer be used for evening worship, add]

Heavenly Father, who slumberest not nor sleepest, we commend to Thy gracious care and keeping ourselves and all that belong to us. We thank Thee for the bright and busy light of day, and now for the softened shadows of the restful night. Lift from our minds the burdens of our wakeful hours;

* Ancient Collect.

visit our bodies with refreshing sleep. Through the darkness keep us safe. And wake us to meet to-morrow's duties in strength of body and vigour of mind, with peace in our spirits and courage in our hearts. Through the grace of our Lord Jesus Christ. Amen.

CIII.—Prayer for Restoration of the Divine Likeness. By Professor W. Gray Elmslie.

O God, who didst make us in Thine image, and hast called us to be perfect, even as our Father in Heaven is perfect, we come to Thee confessing that we have missed our high calling to be Thy children in all goodness, purity, and peace. We have been foolish and passionate, restless, wilful, and disobedient. We have wandered from the ways of heavenly goodness, we have stained the purity of our spirits, we have filled our lives with regrets, fears, and upbraidings, and have lost the true rest of heart and peace of conscience that should have been our joy. But we thank Thee, O Lord, that, in spite of our undesert, Thy blessed Spirit has never forsaken us, and that still, amid our sinning and straying, we hear the voices that stir us to shame and penitence and make within us visions of the things that are honourable and of good report, till all our heart goes out to the heavenly calling, and we long to return to the Father from whom we have wandered, and our spirits are weary of the poor pleasures of sin and the empty pomps and shows of this passing world, with its ceaseless vicissitudes and great unrest.

Holy Father, Thou knowest our wanderings, what they have been; Thine eyes have seen our errors and ignorance and our wrong; Thou knowest our pain and contrition, our craving to be made clean, our longing to be strong and true and good; Thou knowest our tears and struggles, our weakness and our defeats. Thou seest all our helplessness to save ourselves from sin, our incapacity to rise above the bondage of sight and sense, our inability to resist the evil and do the good, and our impotence to recover the gladness of filial trust and the peace of childlike obedience.

O God, Thou art our Father, cleanse us, strengthen Thy children, give us rest. We fling ourselves upon Thy mercy, God of all grace. We appeal to Thy pity, most pitiful Father. We confide ourselves to Thine Omnipotence and invoke Thy sovereign aid. Make Thy strength perfect in our weakness. Take our lives into Thy holy keeping. Mould our hearts according to Thy will, and make us to be in deed and in truth what Thy people ought to be, and Thine shall be the praise and the honour and the glory, world without end. Amen.

CIV.—A Prayer of Invocation. By Professor W. Gray Elmslie.

High and Holy Lord God Almighty, who art the Fountain of all true thoughts and right resolves, be pleased to still the tumult of earthly cares within our breasts, and fill our minds with deep devotion, that for a little while we may rise above the jar and fret of daily life, and join with grateful hearts in that pure worship which, from spirits higher and holier than ours, for ever ascends before Thy throne, giving praise and thanks and honour unto the Lamb that was slain, our Lord and Saviour, Jesus Christ, to whom be glory both now and ever. Amen.

Another Prayer of Invocation (Summer Season). By Professor W. Gray Elmslie.

O God, who hast made this day beautiful with life and warmth and sunshine, be pleased, we beseech Thee, to shine in our hearts with the sunlight of Thy smile, that faith may spring and love unfold, and the waste places of our weary years grow beautiful and bright with blossoms of grace and fruits of goodness that shall be to Thy praise and our joy for evermore. Through Jesus Christ our Lord. Amen.

CV.—A Prayer of Intercession. By Professor W. Gray Elmslie.

Almighty God and Father, who hast taught us to offer prayer to Thee for all men, help us now with brotherly kindness to remember the sorrows and sins of our lost world, so that with pitiful hearts we may make intercession with Thee for our brothers and sisters of the whole human race.

Have mercy, O God, on all mankind; convert the heathen nations to the Cross of Christ; increase the liberality and holy living of Christian peoples; let Christ's kingdom come, and let us and ours be found in Him in that great day when He shall judge the world.

Defend, O Lord, by Thy mighty power, and with Thy counsel guide all Christian kings and righteous rulers of men; especially our Sovereign Lady Queen Victoria and all who, under her, direct the order and administer the government of this great nation.

Bless with light and life from on high the whole Church of Christ; dispel darkness and superstition, worldliness and unbelief; unite all good men in loyalty to Thee and love to one another; and let the truth ever be more fully known and the Master more faithfully served.

Guard our homes from hurt and harm; console friends that mourn; recover any that are sick; bless the little children; cheer the aged, the lonely, and careworn; fulfil the hopes of youth; strengthen those who bear the burdens of maturer years, and bring us all at last to Thy Heavenly home.

Accept these petitions, and the unspoken prayers of our hearts, which we offer one for another for the sake of our Lord Jesus Christ. Amen.

CVI.—**College Prayer. By Benjamin Jowett, M.A., Master of Balliol College.** 1891. *The Master's message to the College in his illness, Sunday, 8th October, 1891, when he was lying between life and death.*

[Being unable, through illness, to preach at the commencement of term, an address, partaking of the nature of a prayer, of which the following is a part, was taken down from his dictation and read by his desire, at the afternoon service.]

. . . At the critical times of life we have not done justice to ourselves. We have not tried enough to see ourselves as we are, or to know the world as it truly is. We have drifted with society, instead of forming independent principles of our own. We have thought too much of ourselves and of what is being said about us. We have cared more for the opinions of others than for the truth. We have not loved others, in all classes of society as Thou, O Lord, hast loved us. We have not thanked Thee sufficiently for the treasures of knowledge, and for the opportunities of doing good, which Thou hast given us in this latter day. We have worried ourselves too much about the religious gossip of the age, and have not consulted enough the fixed forms of truth. We have been indolent and have made many excuses for falling short in Thy work.

And now, O Lord, in these difficult times, when there is a seeming opposition of knowledge and faith, and an accumulation of facts beyond the power of the human mind to conceive, and good men of all religions, more and more meet in Thee; and the strife between classes in society, and between good and evil in our own souls, is not less than of old; and the love of pleasure and the desires of the flesh are always coming in between us and Thee, and we cannot rise above these things to see the light of Heaven but are tossed upon a sea of troubles; we pray Thee be our Guide and Strength and Light, that, looking up to Thee always, we may behold the rock on which we stand, and be confident in the word which Thou hast spoken. . . .

CVII.—A Prayer for Morning or Evening. By Dr. James Martineau. 1891.

The day is Thine, O Lord; the night also is Thine. In the morning we wait on Thee to renew our strength; in the evening to find the shelter of Thy wing. Thou art our Sun; and apart from Thee our toil is blind and weary and there is no glory in our joy. Thou art our Shade; and only when Thou closest round us can our spirits find their rest. Blessed and abiding God! let us not seek Thee far, for Thou art here; but only lay our hearts low before Thee, and Thou wilt enter in.

How long have Thy servants thirsted after Thee, Thou spring of everlasting life? In this land of our home the meditations of ages surround us, and through the treasured thoughts of the wise in many generations we are lifted into a light beyond the solitary soul. Countless are Thy witnesses, Eternal God! the stars without number are but a little part of them, and the prayers and aspirings of every heart of man can never cease to speak Thee. Humbled and blind amid Thy manifold glories, may we find rest in the simplicity of Christ, and be among the pure in heart who alone can see Thee. Save us from feeling after Thee in vain through the darkness of a selfish and unchastened mind.

By Thy tender grace shame away all prejudice and scorn, melt down our pride, quench our fears, sweeten our affections, and lift us above the fretfulness of the world into Thy divine repose. And, O arm of the Lord! awake our slumbering and heedless wills, that we may take all our yoke, and give ourselves up to Thee, not by inward vision only, but by faithful service. As Thou, O Father, workest everlastingly, and not one of Thy blessings ever faileth, may we never grow weary of well-doing; but still follow the steps of Thy beloved Son, to-day and to-morrow, till the sacrifice of ourselves be perfected.

O Thou, whose Word hath appeared full of grace and truth, in our humanity and in the humiliation perfected the holiness of life, more and more let the same mind be in us which was also in Christ Jesus, that we may divest ourselves of every claim, and look for no final peace without the Cross.

By a patient, loving, trustful spirit, steadfast under evil and hopeful of all good, may we rise into ever nearer communion with Thee; and Thou, in Thine own best time, when we are purified by the dews of Thy grace on our repentance, and are prepared for the rest that remaineth, join us at length to the august and saintly company of Thy redeemed.

Hear our suppliant cry O Lord; and have regard to it, not by the measure of our deservings, but according to the fulness of Thy mercy. Amen.

<small>From "Home Prayers." By Rev. James Martineau, D.D. Longmans, Green & Co.</small>

CVIII.—A General Prayer. For a Sunday Morning in Autumn. By the Rev. John Hunter, D.D., Minister of Trinity Church, Glasgow. 1895.

O Thou, who art from everlasting to everlasting, we rest in Thee who dost encompass our passing days with Thine eternity. Take to Thyself now the best we long to utter, yet cannot shape in words, of thankfulness and humility, of aspiration and peace. From many homes we gather, with memories of summer beauties, and autumn gifts of harvest and the glory of the changing leaves, that dwell in our hearts with silent joy even amid the noise of the city and its multitudinous life, its toil, its sins, its suffering, and its endeavour. O give us now Thy blessing as we meet in fellowship before Thee; hallow for us our work by showing us the glory of service in the spirit of Jesus; fit us for more devoted labour, and quicken within us a more patient love.

O Thou All-holy, who minglest Thy thought with ours, we bless Thee for all witness of Thyself.

We thank Thee for law written upon the earth and sky; for marvels and uses of nature; for secrets of truth hidden in the rain-drops and borne on the wings of light; for knowledge that has grown from more to more; for duty that speaks to us with Thine own voice; for joy in common things of home and friendship, which the years deepen and do not exhaust; for moments of insight when we have seen eye to eye with the vision of prophets, and have felt that Thou hast taken us, even us, to be Thy sons. Father, we thank Thee for blessed help through communion, not only with high and heroic souls, but with each other, as we have sought Thee together in the house of prayer; we bless Thee for seasons of worship when we have laid aside our care, and the burden of life has been lifted and hope has been renewed; we thank Thee that Thou hast sometimes given us the deep joy of knowing that through our word Thy Spirit has helped and comforted some struggling, suffering soul. O God, who dost reveal Thyself in so many ways, accept us, and as we live and move and have our being in Thee, teach us the awful mystery that Thou dost live and move in and through us. Yet with thankfulness must linger likewise confession. Too often has our sight been dim and our hearts cold; we have seen the best with dull and distant vision, and we have not loved it; forgive us, Father, if we have rashly sought to open blind eyes while we ourselves saw not; if we have striven to unstop deaf ears while our own were sealed. O give us a clearer vision and a more steadfast will. Save us from false judgment of others through rash conceit and an unloving pride; save us from the indolence which shrinks from labour, and the carelessness which takes no heed of great issues; save us from fear which will not grapple with problems that may be too hard for us; save us from the languor and weariness that too often numb our best efforts, and the spirit of complaint that the reward is not ours. O give us of the lowliness and the love of Christ; teach us humility; awaken us from sloth; may we have more of the spirit of true sacrifice, that time and strength, thought and hope, may be given freely, ungrudgingly, with a constant joy, for the truth's sake and our brethren's sake in Thee.

So, gracious Father, draw us closer to each other for fellow-work and cheer. Strengthen our hearts and hands with common trust; in difficulty uphold us that we may not be daunted; in lowliness sustain us with Thy sympathy. More and more may we find new might in Thee, that the truth that is in us may overcome indifference or dislike;

more and more may we fulfil the word of Jesus and be known as His disciples through mutual love. And then hasten the time when all that divides the churches shall disappear, and all who seek after righteousness shall strive together, that government may be just, and teaching wise, and commerce equitable, and labour faithful, and all our life be set in harmony with Thy perfect law. So may Thy kingdom come on earth as it is in Heaven. Amen.

From "Devotional Services for Public Worship." By the Rev. John Hunter, D.D. J. McLehose & Sons, Glasgow.

CIX.—A Prayer for the use of the Young People of a Household. 1894.

O Lord God, our Heavenly Father, Thou who dwellest everywhere, who seest everything, who knowest all the thoughts and intents of the heart, we cannot hide anything from Thee, and we would not if we could. We know how glad we have felt when, if we have done wrong to an earthly friend, we have gone to him and told him our fault and obtained his forgiveness. How much greater, then, is our joy when we hear Thee speak to us the word of pardon! Father, we have sinned against Thee, and done evil in Thy sight; we have not set Thee always before us; we have wandered away from

Thee and Thy holy counsels; we have done many things that we ought not to have done, and we come to Thee for pardon. Help us not only to say these words with our lips, but to feel them in our hearts. May our sense of having done evil things in Thy sight be as real to us as when our consciences tell us we have done wrong to our fellow-creatures. And, just as we feel that we cannot meet them, or talk to them, or open our hearts to them, until we have confessed our wrong-doing, so may we feel when we have transgressed against Thee. And we know that all wrong done to our fellows is wrong done to Thee, for Thou lovest all. So we come to Thee this day and desire to tell Thee all our faults, in thought and word and deed, and to beg Thy forgiveness; for we know that, if we confess our sins, Thou art faithful and just to forgive us our sins and to cleanse us from all unrighteousness.

Help us, O Lord, to hate sin, which separates us from Thee, and hinders us from walking in the ways of true pleasantness and peace that Thou wouldst have us choose. Shield us in the midst of temptation, for Thou, who wast once a child and youth as we are, hast been tempted in all points like as we have; keep us in daily contact with things that are pure and honest, and lovely, and of good report; lead us into the beautiful places of life where Thou thyself art always to be found, and give to us the blessing of the pure in heart, so that, everywhere and in all things, we may see God.

We ask Thee, O Lord, to keep us in all our ways; to help us to fight the battle of life always on the side of truth and purity, of honour and right; to be with us in our going out and our coming in; to strengthen us in hours of weakness and indecision, and to restrain us in hours of too great joy; to guide us in all our studies, so that in after life we may employ our knowledge for the good of others; to take away everything that would mar our lives and hinder us from loving Thee as the great and good Father of Mankind, who lovest all.

Be pleased, O Lord, to accept our thanks for all that Thou hast done for us; for home and home-delights, for parents, relations, and friends; for food and raiment, for books and pictures, for birds and flowers, for everything that makes life beautiful and fair. And we would thank Thee for every victory over temper and temptation, for every opportunity of saying and doing that which our hearts tell us would please Thee, for every disappointment, trial, or vexation which we have overcome. May these things make us stronger to do Thy will. Above all, we thank Thee, Thou Good Shepherd of the sheep, that Thou dost lead us forth. Whether it be by dangerous pathways, or in dark valleys, or on the hill-tops of life bathed in sunshine, help us to keep close to Thy side; teach us how to listen, in the midst of the world's confusion, to the faintest whisper of Thy voice; and in heart and thought, in word and purpose, make us Thine own.

And to Him who is able to keep us from falling, and to present us faultless before the presence of His glory with exceeding joy, be all the praise and glory for ever and ever. Amen.

From "Truth in Story." (Hodder Brothers.)

CX.—A Little Child's Prayer.

O Lord Jesus Christ, suffer a little child to come unto Thee. Though I am very young, yet I have done wrong against Thee. Create in me a clean heart, O God, and put a right spirit within me. I am ignorant, Lord teach me; I am weak, Lord help me, and guide me into the ways of Heaven, that at last I may go where all good children go, and dwell with Thee for ever and ever. Amen.

Please God, bless father and mother [grandpapa, grandmama, uncles, and aunts], and all kind friends and relations.

And pray, God, bless me, and make me a good little boy [girl] for Jesus' sake. Amen.

Jesus, tender Shepherd, hear me,
    Bless Thy little lamb to-night,
Through the darkness be Thou near me,
    Keep me safe till morning light. Amen.

CXI.—Prayer for the Queen. By the Chaplain of the American Senate. MAY 26, 1897.

["In opening the proceedings of the Senate to-day (May 26th, 1897) the Blind Chaplain prayed for the Queen in the words given below. The prayer was ordered to be printed in full in the Official Journal—a very rare proceeding."—*Morning Newspaper.*]

O Thou, who art King of Kings and Lord of Lords, we bless Thee for the long and illustrious reign of Thy Servant, the gracious sovereign lady Queen Victoria, whose conduct and character as daughter, wife, and mother, as well as illustrious Sovereign, have enshrined her in the hearts and reverence of true-hearted men and women around the world. So endow and guide the councils of that realm, and of our own beloved country, that hand in hand they may tread the path of conservative progress to the goal of Christian civilisation, until the Prince of the Kings of the earth, the first begotten from the dead, shall become monarch of all hearts and all lives in our race. Amen.

Alphabetical List of Authors.

ANDREWES, Bishop Lancelot, 55, 58
Aquinas, St. Thomas, 36
Arnold, Dr. Thomas, 123
Arnold, Matthew, 136
Augustine, St., 29

BASIL, St., 31, 32
Baxter, Richard, 78
Beecher, Rev. H. W., 178
Behmen, Jacob, 65
Böhme, Jacob, 65
Bowring, Sir John, 139
Bradwardine, Archbishop Thomas, 38
Browning, E. B., 125
Burn, John, 114

CALVIN, John, 46, 47, 49, 50
Chalmers, Dr. Thomas, 129, 131
Chaplain of American Senate, 225
Charles I., 72
Chatterton, Thomas, 118
Cobbe, Miss F. P., 166
Colet, John, 42
Colonna, Vittoria, 53, 54
Cook, Eliza, 151

DAMASCENUS, John, 33
Doddridge, Dr. Philip, 102
Donne, Dr. John, 82, 84
Drummond of Hawthornden, 77
Dykes, Dr. J. Oswald, 187

ELIZABETH, Queen, 71
Elmslie, Professor W. G., 206, 210, 212, 213

FLETCHER, Dr. Alexander, 144
Forbes, Principal, 143

GRANT, Sir Robert, 121

HALL, Bishop, 64
Heber, Bishop Reginald, 141
Herbert, George, 70
Herrick, Robert, 68
Hinton, Dr. James, 162
Hunter, Dr. John, 218

JAMES, St., 25
Jerome, St., 26
John Damascenus, 33
Johnson, Dr. Samuel, 103, 104, 105
Jonson, Ben, 62
Jowett, Professor Benjamin, 214

KEMPIS, Thomas á, 39
Ken, Bishop, 91
King Charles I., 72
Knill, Rev. Richard, 142
Knox, John, 44

LACORDAIRE, Abbé, 150
Lassenius, Johann, 89
Laud, Archbishop, 61
Law, William, 101
Lawrence, Sir Henry, 153
Layman, A, 221, 224
Lowell, J. R., 150
Luther, Martin, 51

MANT, Bishop Richard, 120
Martineau, Dr. James, 216
Metaphrastes, Simeon, 35
Moore, Thomas, 121
Moravian Litany, 106
Monod, Rev. Adolphe, 140

Alphabetical List of Authors.

PARKER, Dr. Joseph, 203, 205
Pascal, Blaise, 81
Peel, Sir Robert, 152
Polycarp, St., 24
Pope, Alexander, 111
Prince Imperial of France, 168
Pusey, Dr. E. B., 154

QUARLES, Francis, 86, 88
Queen Elizabeth, 71

RALEIGH, Sir Walter, 54
Rykman, Andrew, 95

SCHOOL BOARD, First London, 163
Service, Dr. John, 193, 200
Shaftesbury, Seventh Earl of, 190
Sheppard, Mr. John, 158, 160
  ,,   Mrs. John, 133
Southey, Robert, 119
Spurgeon, Rev. C. H., 170
St. Augustine, 29

St. Basil, 31, 32
St. Francis Xavier, 45
St. James, 25
St. Jerome, 26
St. Polycarp, 24
St. Thomas Aquinas, 36

TAYLOR, Jeremy, 74, 76
Tersteegen, Gerhard, 107, 108
Thomas Aquinas, 36
Thomas à Kempis, 39
Thornton, Henry, 147

VAUGHAN, Henry, 93

WESLEY, Charles, 116
Wesley, Susanna, 117
Whittier, J. G., 95, 124
Wilson, Bishop, 94
Wotton, Sir Henry, 60

XAVIER, St. Francis, 45

Subject Index.

Adoration, 45, 108, 117

Bereavement, 121, 200

Child's Prayer, A, 224
Collects, 31, 32
Communion (before), 26, 36, 49, 105
Confession, 50
Contrition, 33, 65, 140, 160
Conversion, 141

Divine Guidance in Dispensing Gifts, 102
Divine Guidance, 86, 140, 152
Doubt, 104, 160

"Elixir, The," 70
Evening, 47, 58, 89, 151

Faith, 158
Family Use, 42, 46, 47, 61, 72, 89, 91, 123, 139, 144, 147, 187, 203, 205, 206, 221
Friendship, 129

General, 25, 42, 46, 47, 76, 78, 91, 106, 109, 111, 170, 178, 187, 193, 206, 210, 212, 213, 218
Grace, 58, 74, 160, 166

Historical, 24, 35, 44, 51, 71, 72, 106, 131, 133, 152, 163, 168, 225

Hymns of Prayer, 54, 84, 93, 116, 119, 124, 136, 139

Litanies, 68, 82, 106, 120, 121
Liturgies, 25, 49, 50, 78

Mercy, 77
Missions, 106
Morning, 46, 55, 144, 147, 153, 154, 216

Peace, 29, 39, 124
Preparation, 103, 107, 143, 150, 153
Private Use, 26, 38, 50, 55, 58, 62, 64, 65, 75, 81, 84, 88, 94, 95, 101, 104, 116, 119, 120, 123, 150, 153, 154, 158, 190

Resignation, 118
Rest in God, 29

Self-dedication, 107, 114
Shaftesbury, Prayers of Lord, 190
Sickness (in time of), 60, 81, 84, 143, 150, 151
Spiritual Life, 53, 54, 166
Supplication, 125, 136, 160, 211

Thanksgiving, 91
Thoughts on Prayer, 1, 5, 8, 13, 15, 19, 162
Times and Seasons, 142, 143, 187

www.ingramcontent.com/pod-product-compliance
Lightning Source LLC
Chambersburg PA
CBHW031745230426
43669CB00007B/489